The Catholic Church in the Twenty-first Century

Finding Hope for Its Future in the Wisdom of Its Past

A Symposium With Rev. Daniel J. Harrington, S.J.,
Rev. Michael J. Buckley, S.J., Dr. Catherine M. Mooney,
Rev. Thomas F. O'Meara, O.P., Rev. Michael J. Himes,
Dr. Richard R. Gaillardetz

Editor: Rev. Michael J. Himes

Liguori
LIGUORI, MISSOURI

Imprimi Potest:
Richard Thibodeau, C.Ss.R.
Provincial, Denver Province
The Redemptorists

ISBN 0-7648-1147-9
Library of Congress Catalog Card Number: 2003114960

© 2004, Catholic Community Foundation
Printed in the United States of America
08 07 06 05 04   5 4 3 2 1

Scripture quotations are from the *New Revised Standard Version of the Bible,* © 1989 by the Division of Christian Education of the National Council of Churches of Christ in the USA. Used with permission. All rights reserved.

To order, call 1-800-325-9521
www.liguori.org
www.catholicbooksonline.com

The
Catholic Church
in the
Twenty-First Century

Contents

Preface

On May 31, 2003, over five hundred people—bishops, an abbot, monks, priests, lay women and men, religious men and women, and parish ministers—gathered to hear an extraordinary panel of theologians explore the history of the Church through the lens of the gifts and lessons for the Church today that are in that story.

Held at the Jesuit Rockhurst High School in Kansas City, Missouri, it was a collaboration of many committed Catholics. Primarily under the leadership and sponsorship of Bernadette and Richard Miller and with the help of Michael J. Himes, Michael J. Buckley, S.J. and Richard Miller II, scholars were gathered. Bishop Raymond Boland of the diocese of Kansas City, MO, and his staff cooperated and worked to make the event successful, as did the faculty and staff at Rockhurst High School. The members of the Catholic Community Foundation also supported the endeavor.

At the end of the day, eyes and hearts and minds were opened, energy was high and the conversation was about how to make these extraordinary talks, and those of next year's event, available to the larger Church. Thus it is that Liguori Publications is making available this symposium in a book which contains the talks and a panel discussion based on questions from the audience. The symposium is also available in sets of video and audio tapes accompanied by a study guide written by Jean Marie Hiesberger. To order the videos, audio tapes, extra copies of the study guide, and/or the book, please call 1-800-325-9521 or fax 1-800-325-9526.

Introduction

Problems and Challenges in the Contemporary Church

Richard W. Miller II, Ph.D. Candidate in Theology, Boston College

On December 21, 2001, unbeknownst to Boston Catholics who were preparing to celebrate Christmas, a Massachusetts Appeals Court ruled in favor of the Boston Globe. The ruling required that thousands of documents, which had been under a confidentiality seal in the eighty-six sexual molestation lawsuits against former priest John Geoghan, be made public.[1] These documents told the unimaginably shocking story of a priest using the authority and trust that his Roman collar conferred upon him to ingratiate himself to single parent families in order to rape and molest their children. Yet, it was the account these documents gave of the actions and inactions of Church leaders that would trigger perhaps the greatest crisis in the history of the Catholic Church in the United States.

For thirty years, the Archdiocese of Boston, in effect, multiplied the number of victims into the hundreds by buying the silence of the victim's families through confidential settlements and by moving the priest to other unsuspecting parishes providing him with more potential victims.

Though John Geoghan was a particularly heinous example, it became clear—as stories began to pour out in newspapers across the country and around the world—that there was a pattern among church leaders of covering up the crimes of predator priests through confidential settlements only to reassign them to new positions where they would inevitably upend the lives of innocent children.

Had the Boston Globe not followed the story of John Geoghan into the courts, the documents would never have been released and children in other dioceses across the country would still be in danger of being abused. Without the secular press, the American Catholic

---

1. "Church Leaders' Depositions to Be Made Public: Boston Archdiocese Loses Court Appeal in Geoghan Abuse Case," *Boston Globe*, 25 December 2001, third edition.

Church would not have been pressured to reform itself, and we would not today have a National Sex Abuse Policy like the one drafted in Dallas in June 2002. The sad fact is that the Church came close to reform seventeen years and hundreds of victims earlier, in 1985, when clergy and other legal and mental health experts brought to the National Conference of Catholic Bishops a comprehensive plan to deal with the looming problem. That document's prophetic warnings, however—of the lack of any known cure for pedophilia and the need to move quickly and responsibly to address "the single most serious and far reaching problem facing our Church today,"[2]—fell on deaf ears.

The sexual abuse crisis in the Catholic Church has had profound consequences beyond the trauma inflicted on the victims. The moral authority of the Church in the wider society has been considerably compromised. Record numbers of Catholics in the United States feel increasingly alienated from the Church and its leadership. Some are voting with their feet by choosing to no longer attend Mass. Still more are voting with their pocketbooks by no longer giving to a Church they do not trust. The words of Bernard Cardinal Law, who played a central role in the scandal in Boston, perhaps best describe the present Church climate in the wake of the sexual abuse scandal: "Betrayal hangs like a heavy cloud over the Church today…a betrayal of trust is at the heart of the evil in the sexual abuse of children by clergy."[3]

---

2. F. Ray Mouton, J.D., Rev. Thomas P. Doyle, O.P., J.C.D., Rev. Michael Peterson, M.D., "The Problem of Sexual Molestation by Roman Catholic Clergy: Meeting the Problem in a Comprehensive and Responsible Manner" (presented to the National Conference of Catholic Bishops, Washington, D.C., 1985), p. 92.

3. The Investigative Staff of The Boston Globe, *Betrayal: The Crisis in the Catholic Church.* (Boston: Little, Brown, and Company, 2002; Boston: First Back Bay, 2003), p. 4. It should be noted that this statement from Cardinal Law has been taken out of context. I have used his words as a poignant *description of the experience of the faithful* who feel betrayed not simply by the abusive priests, but, more importantly, by those bishops who for years shuttled abusive priests from parish to parish. Cardinal Law, however, in his Good Friday letter of 2002, was not referring to himself or other bishops, who shuttled abusive priests from parish to parish, as "betrayers of trust." His letter suggests that only the abusive priests had earned such a title.

While this cloud pervades the present ecclesial climate, it is not the only challenge on the horizon. The growing shortage of priests, an increasingly involved and outspoken laity, and the difficult balancing act between the need to maintain the unity of the Church while recognizing that the Church is really a world Church, represent some of the serious challenges facing the Church today.

The shortage of priests is an ever growing problem. Worldwide, the ratio of priests—including both diocesan and religious priests—to faithful has dropped by 63 percent between 1969 and 1998. In the United States, there has been a 59 percent decrease in the ratio of the number of priests to the total number of Catholics in the same period. In Europe, there has been a 22 percent decrease,[4] and in Central and South America, the ratio of priests to Catholics has dropped 80 percent. While some have trumpeted the growth of priestly vocations in Africa, which have increased by 57 percent from 1969 to 1998, this statistic has to be understood in the context of the actual number of Catholics these priests are called to serve. Because of the over 200 percent increase in the number of Catholics in Africa during the same period, the ratio of priests to Catholics overall has actually decreased by nearly 75 percent.[5] The result is that many communities in Africa have to wait weeks or even months before a priest can visit to celebrate Sunday Eucharist.

There is even more striking statistical data that bears directly on the Church in the United States. In 2000, there were 427 diocesan

---

4. While Europe has the lowest percentage of decrease in the ratio of priests to Catholics of any of the major Catholic regions of the world, this is because the Catholic population in Europe has the lowest percentage of growth (9 percent) of any of the major Catholic regions of the world, 1969-1998. In fact, Europe has had the greatest percentage decline (16 percent) of priests of any of the major Catholic regions of the world, 1969-1998.

5. All statistics in this paragraph are calculated from data obtained from the following two sources: Frank Pycroft, *Catholic Facts and Figures* (London: Sheed & Ward, 1977); Monsignor Formenti and Enrico Neena, "Worldwide Statistics, 1998" in *The Official Catholic Directory, Anno Domini 2001, Part II*, eds. Eileen Fanning, Sumitra B. Ramaprasad, Daniel D. Crawford, and Linda Hummer (New Providence, New Jersey: P.J. Kennedy & Sons in association with National Register Publishing, 2001), pp. 219-229.

ordinations, but 630 diocesan priests died and 85 left the priest-hood.[6] Thus in 2000, the U.S. Church lost a total of 288 diocesan priests. It should not then come as a complete surprise that in the U.S. Catholic Church as of 2002, one out of every seven parishes did not have a resident priest.[7] In addition, demographic data suggests that in the next ten to fifteen years the situation will become considerably worse. In 1999, nearly one out of every four priests in the U.S. Church was retired, sick, or otherwise not actively engaged in full-time pastoral ministry.[8] Of the diocesan priests active in ministry in 1999, the average age was fifty-nine, with 15 percent over seventy-four, 22 percent between sixty-five and seventy-four, and another 22 percent between the ages of fifty-five and sixty-four.[9]

The shortage of priests has contributed to the emergence of an increasingly involved and outspoken laity. Because of the shortage of priests over the last thirty years, the day-to-day life of many parishes is increasingly managed and run by lay people. In addition, the laity in the developed world has become more outspoken and demanded greater responsibility in recent decades, largely because the laity is better educated than ever before. For most of the Church's history the priest was the most educated person in the community, with the population being predominantly illiterate. That is no longer the case. During the past seventy years in the United States, there has been a dramatic shift in the education level of Catholics. This can be seen in the extraordinary shift in the overall education level

---

6. Secretaria Status Rationarium Generale Ecclesiae, *Annuarium Statisticum Ecclesiae/ Statistical Yearbook of the Church/Annuaire Statistique de L'Eglise 2000* (Vatican City: Libreria Editrice Vaticana, 2002).

7. This statistic is calculated from data provided by the Center for Applied Research in the Apostolate (CARA), "Frequently Requested Church Statistics" at http://cara.georgetown.edu/bulletin/index.htm. (Washington, D.C.: Georgetown University, 2002).

8. Center for Applied Research in the Apostolate (CARA), *Catholicism USA: A Portrait of the Catholic Church in the United States*, eds. Bryan T. Froehle and Mary L. Gautier (Maryknoll, New York: Orbis Books, 2000), p. 115.

9. Ibid., p. 112.

of the wider U.S. population. In 1940, more than 50 percent of the U.S. population aged twenty-five and older had no more than an eighth-grade education.[10] By the year 2000, "84 percent of the population 25 years old and over had completed high school, and 26 percent had completed four or more years of college."[11] It should, therefore, come as no surprise that in the wake of the sex abuse scandal in the Boston Archdiocese, the largest U.S. grass-roots lay organization, Voice of the Faithful, emerged out of an affluent, highly educated parish in the suburbs, and was founded by a world renowned cardiologist. Some have condemned Voice of the Faithful while others have welcomed it, but whatever one thinks of this group, one would have to recognize that defining the role of the laity is an important challenge in the days ahead.

As I have presented the problems of the sex abuse scandal, the priest shortage, and the challenge of defining a role for the laity, most of us have naturally heard and understood these problems in terms of our distinctive experience as American Catholics. The Church, however, is a world Church—the U.S. Church represents only 6 percent of the total world Catholic population. Though the Church throughout the world faces a priest shortage, many of the problems and challenges in the U.S. Church are quite different from the Church in Africa or India or even in Central America, where they all have their own particular problems and challenges. For instance, a highly educated and outspoken laity is not a challenge in the African Church where literacy rates and educational levels are significantly lower than in the U.S. The African Church, on the other hand, faces the challenge of transplanting Catholic teaching firmly rooted in the soil of Western culture and Western thought forms into the soil of African native religions, which are not immediately

---

10. U.S. Department of Education, National Center for Education Statistics, *120 Years of American Education: A Statistical Portrait*, ed. Thomas D. Snyder (Washington, D.C.: National Center for Education Statistics, 1993), p. 7.

11. U.S. Department of Education, National Center for Education Statistics, *Digest of Education Statistics, 2001*, by Thomas D. Snyder (Washington, D.C.: National Center for Education Statistics, 2002), p. 6.

hospitable to such transplantation. The task is daunting because "…there is not much support in African culture for a celibate clergy, canon law, or the doctrinal distinctions developed through centuries of debates by European theologians."[12] How, then, is the Church going to remain one Church while at the same time effectively performing its ministry in cultures and contexts as different as the United States and sub-Saharan Africa?

The sex abuse scandal, the growing shortage of priests, determining the role of an increasingly involved and outspoken laity, and the difficult balancing act between the need to maintain the unity of the Church while recognizing that the Church is truly a world Church, represent some of the serious challenges facing the Church today. In light of this enumeration of some of the serious problems and challenges facing the contemporary Church, many of you—sensitive to truth in advertising—might be asking yourself: "Where is the hope?"

I have two initial reasons for hope. The first is found in the format of the papers presented here. Some Catholics find hope and comfort in the idea that while everything else around them changes, the Church is the one thing you can count on because it never changes. But if this were true, there would not be much hope for the future Church. If the Church were of its very nature immutable, and thus unable to change, we would not be able to take the necessary steps to recover the moral authority of the Church after the sex abuse scandal, we would just have to live with less and less priests while the talents and gifts of the laity would forever be restricted to their present role, and the Church could never respond to the demands and challenges presented by its rapid growth in the third world. If the Church cannot of its very nature change, then all we could do in the face of the present challenges is close our eyes and hold on tighter to our sinking ship. The hope this conference wants to convey in addressing the future of the Church in terms of the

---

12. Thomas J. Reese, *Inside the Vatican: The Politics and Organization of the Catholic Church* (Cambridge, Massachusetts: Harvard University Press, 1996), p. 273.

wisdom of its past lies in the fact that, from the age of the New Testament until Vatican II and today—the Church *has* changed, and thus the Church both can and must continue to change in order to flourish in its preaching, teaching, and sacramental ministries.

The second reason for hope is the setting of this conference in the diocese of Kansas City, MO, and the way in which it has come to fruition. Here you have a diocese that has not had a sex abuse scandal. In addition, the idea of bringing together some of the best theological minds available to deal with central issues facing the Church in the twenty-first century emerged from a lay leader in the community, was funded and supported by nearly a hundred other Catholic lay and religious leaders in the community, the local colleges, and, perhaps most significantly, enthusiastically supported by Bishop Boland and his staff, who took charge of all the publicity, without which this conference would not have been possible.

1. What Can We Learn From the Church in the New Testament?

Rev. Daniel J. Harrington, S.J., Weston Jesuit School of Theology

What can the Church of the twenty-first century learn from the Church of the first century? I have been asking and trying to answer this question in my teaching and preaching since the turn of the millennium. The question has become ever more urgent. By now, the apocalyptic predictions about the Y2K computer scare seem like a pleasant memory. Meanwhile, the terrorist attacks of September 11, 2001, the Catholic priest sexual abuse crisis (whose epicenter is my hometown of Boston), the *Enron*™ and other business scandals, and the war in Iraq have come upon us one after another, and left most of us confused and afraid. The bright promises of the new millennium have faded quickly.

For many years, I have had the privilege of studying, teaching, and preaching Scripture. I have found the Bible to be an inexhaustible resource of spiritual insight and challenge. In the setting where I live, the priest sexual abuse crisis hangs over the city like a dark and poisonous cloud. Nevertheless, as business people like to say, every problem is an opportunity. And so in my teaching and preaching I keep returning to the question: "What can the Church of the twenty-first century, in our current crises, learn from the Church of the first century?"

I want to reflect on seven things that we can learn from the New Testament in our present crisis. I will focus on Paul's letters because they are the earliest written documents in the New Testament, from the 50s of what we call the first Christian century. Along the way I will also refer to some other New Testament texts.

Recognize That Crisis Is Not a New Phenomenon in the Church

One of our local television stations, whenever it runs a story involving the Catholic Church, flashes on the screen a logo that says,

"Crisis in the Church." The assumption seems to be that putting together the words "crisis" and "Church" is something unprecedented, like "breaking news." But the New Testament is full of cases of crisis in the Church. The first Christian century was not an untroubled "golden age" for the Church. Indeed, by facing and resolving these crises the early Church made its greatest progress.

Let me list a few crises from the pages of the New Testament: When is the Lord coming, and what about those who die before he comes (1 Thessalonians)? Do Gentiles have to become Jews in order to be real Christians (Galatians)? Can Christians trust the gospel preached by Paul (Philippians, 2 Corinthians)? Can non-Jews be part of the people of God (Romans)? Can Christians participate in civil religious ceremonies associated with worship of the Roman emperor and the goddess Roma (Revelation)?

If you want to see striking examples of crisis in the Church, above all read Paul's First Letter to the Corinthians. Corinth was a port city in Greece, not far from Athens. Paul had founded and shaped the Christian community at Corinth. As was his custom, Paul then moved on to found other Christian communities. The letters of Paul included in our New Testament were occasional communications from the founding apostle that gave theological advice on pastoral problems which had arisen in his absence.

Consider the issues that Paul addressed in First Corinthians: factions of Christians dividing themselves according to the apostles who brought them to Christian faith (Paul, Apollo, or Cephas, i.e., Peter), the countenancing of sexual immorality on the grounds that "all things are lawful for me," lawsuits between fellow Christians being brought to civil courts, debates over the relative value of celibacy and marriage, clashes between Christian groups known as the "strong" and the "weak," socioeconomic and liturgical abuses at the celebration of the Eucharist and at the assemblies of the community, the importance of speaking in tongues, and (of course) money given to the collection. All this in the mid-50s of the first Christian century!

Does all this sound familiar? One New Testament scholar has

pronounced that every problem facing the Church today can be found in some form in Paul's First Letter to the Corinthians. In any case, it is clear from First Corinthians and other New Testament writings that crisis is not a new phenomenon in the Church.

Acknowledge That Sin Is Not a New Phenomenon in the Church

Early Christians were an enthusiastic group. They were convinced that Jesus' death and resurrection had changed everything. They believed that Jesus' death on the cross had wiped away sin's ultimate power over humans and opened up the way to a new relationship with God. And they believed that the resurrection of Jesus meant that the kingdom of God had been inaugurated and that they lived in a "new creation."

One of Paul's major tasks as a founding apostle and a pastoral theologian was to emphasize the positive effects of the Christ-event (Jesus' life, death, and resurrection) in the present, and to remind Christians that the fullness of God's kingdom is still future. In other words, through Christ, God's kingdom is both already and not yet. And the "not yet" dimension is made manifest in the sins committed by Christians.

In the earliest New Testament document—1 Thessalonians, written around A.D. 51—Paul had to warn Christians in a community that he had founded not to exploit others sexually and especially not to draw fellow Christians into *porneia,* which here (1 Thessalonians 4:3-6) is usually translated as "fornication." In 1 Corinthians 5:1-2, we hear about a man who was living with his father's wife. She was most likely his stepmother or his father's concubine. Such an arrangement was forbidden both in the Old Testament and in Roman law. And some Christians at Corinth were apparently consorting with prostitutes and justifying it under the slogan "all things are lawful for me" (6:12).

To such self-deluded persons, Paul issued the retort: "but not all things are beneficial." What Paul meant is that such actions are totally inappropriate for those who are members of the body of Christ and whose bodies are temples of the Holy Spirit (6:15,19). Instead, such actions are manifestations of the perduring presence of sin and death in the world. While Christ has already won the ultimate victory over sin and death, there remain battles to be fought before the fullness of God's kingdom comes. Sin is down, but not out.

Paul and other early Christians were both idealists and realists. They joyfully celebrated the liberation and the revelation that they had experienced in and through Christ. Nevertheless, they recognized the continuing presence of sin in the world and even in the Church as an indication that much more needed to take place before God's will would be done on earth as it is in heaven. Sin is not a new phenomenon in the Church.

Focus on Jesus' Death and Resurrection as the Core of Christian Faith

The link between sin and Jesus' death is part of the earliest summaries of Christian faith. What Paul describes as the gospel that he had received and handed on to the Corinthians proclaims first of all: "Christ died for our sins" (1 Corinthians 15:3). Here, and elsewhere in the New Testament (especially in Hebrews), the death of Jesus is given a sacrificial interpretation. As the perfect sin offering, Jesus made possible a new relationship of intimacy with God. Paul's theology has been aptly described as a soteriological Christology insofar as it is primarily concerned with the saving effects of Jesus' death and resurrection: freedom, salvation, justification, redemption, sanctification, access to God, and so forth.

What we are talking about here is often called the paschal mystery. In trying to resolve or at least shed light on the various crises that his communities faced, Paul always comes back to the example of Jesus, not so much to his specific teachings or his miracles, but rather to his death and resurrection.

Here are some examples. To exhort the Thessalonian Christians to show courage in the face of persecution, Paul puts forward the example of "the Lord Jesus and the prophets" (1 Thessalonians 2:15). When the Galatian community was being torn apart about whether the Gentiles there had to become Jews, Paul emphasized Jesus Christ as the true descendant of Abraham and proclaimed that people of faith are all "one in Christ Jesus" and so Abraham's "children" (Galatians 3:28-29). In writing to the Philippians, urging them to greater union, mutual respect, and humility, Paul invokes an early Christian hymn that reminds us that Christ Jesus "emptied himself, taking the form of a slave, being born in human likeness" (Philippians 2:7).

When Paul urged the Corinthians to give generously to the collection for their fellow Christians in Jerusalem, he appealed to Christ, who "though he was rich, yet for your sakes he became poor, so that by his poverty you might become rich" (2 Corinthians 8:9). Finally, Paul refers to the Eucharist, or Lord's Supper, only twice in his letters (1 Corinthians 10:14-21; 11:17-34). In both cases he does so in order to bring the paschal mystery celebrated in the Eucharist to bear on religious and socioeconomic crises facing the Corinthian Christians. In dealing with crises, Paul keeps bringing himself and his fellow Christians back to Jesus' death and resurrection as the core of Christian faith.

Remember That Forgiveness and Reconciliation Are Always Possible

One of the problems in the recent priest sexual abuse crisis has been premature or too easy talk about forgiveness and reconciliation. Where our sense of sin is weak, the meaning of terms such as forgiveness and reconciliation also becomes attenuated. But that is no excuse for ignoring them.

The earliest professions of Christian faith that we have proclaim that "Christ died for our sins," and when Paul came to describe the ministry of Christ, as well as his own ministry, he did so in terms of reconciliation: "In Christ God was reconciling the world to himself, not counting their trespasses against them, and entrusting the message of reconciliation to us" (2 Corinthians 5:19). The early Christian hymn about Christ as the Wisdom of God (see Colossians 1:15-20) describes Christ's reconciling work in cosmic terms: "through him God was pleased to reconcile to himself all things, whether on earth or in heaven, by making peace through the blood of his cross" (1:20). Forgiveness of sins and reconciliation are at the heart of the Christian message.

In some cases Paul made himself an agent of reconciliation within Christian communities. In adjudicating the dispute about eating food blessed at pagan temples or by pagan priests in 1 Corinthians 8—10, Paul pleads for sensitivity on both sides to the consciences of others. And in the controversies over foods and holy days in Romans 14—15, Paul recommends that both sides leave the final judgment to God.

However, in treating the egregious offense of the incestuous man in 1 Corinthians 5:1-5, Paul demands that the offender and his supporters come to recognize and acknowledge his sin. He recommends that a public process of excommunication be initiated by the community. The positive goal seems to be to shock the offender into recognition and confession so that "his spirit may be saved in the day of the Lord" (5:5). I take this to mean "so that the process of forgiveness and reconciliation might begin before it is too late." The process that Paul recommends is analogous to the three-step procedure taken over from Judaism and described in Matthew 18:15-17. That description is followed, in Matthew 18:21-35, by the parable of the unforgiving servant, which warns against putting limits on our willingness to forgive one another.

Face the Fact of Scandal in Our Church

By trying to cover up scandal, the Catholic Church has involved itself in even greater scandal. The result has been a terrible loss of credibility and moral authority in the general public and among its own members.

The word "scandal" is a New Testament word. It derives from the Greek *skandalon*, whose root sense is "obstacle, roadblock, trap." There is, however, some ambiguity surrounding this term. "Scandal" can refer to something that causes offense or revulsion, and results in opposition, disapproval, or hostility. This is the sense that

Paul evokes when he speaks paradoxically about the scandal of the cross in 1 Corinthians 1—4. The greatest scandal facing early Christians was the fact that their hero, Jesus of Nazareth, was crucified under Pontius Pilate. He died as a criminal in a Roman mode of execution reserved for rebels and slaves. How is this scandal to be explained? Rather than mounting a defense, Paul embraces the cross as the mysterious wisdom of God and glories in the fact that "we proclaim Christ crucified, a stumbling block (*skandalon*) to Jews and foolishness to Gentiles" (1 Corinthians 1:23). The cross was and is the greatest Christian scandal.

There is another way to understand "scandal" in the New Testament. That way takes scandal as actions or circumstances that lead others into sin, or at least into actions contrary to their beliefs or customary ways of action (ethics). Paul uses the term in that sense in Romans 16:17, and the same sense underlies the gospel sayings about tempting or scandalizing others (as in Mark 10:42-48). This is the definition of scandal used in the *Catechism of the Catholic Church,* and we can use this sense to talk about the roots of the priest sexual abuse scandal.

A third dimension to "scandal" in the New Testament may be captured by the question, "What will outsiders think of us?" This notion comes out most explicitly in 1 Corinthians 6:1-11, where Paul expresses outrage at situations in which one Christian files a lawsuit against another Christian and has it resolved before a civil court and a non-Christian judge. Paul's concerns are both the good public reputation of the Christian community and the inability of Christians to resolve disputes among themselves.

As events have unfolded over the past year and a half, I have often reflected on Paul's advice in 1 Corinthians 6, and have seen in it the roots of the scandal in which criminal activity by one Christian upon another was covered up, with the result that even more criminal activity was made possible. However, before blaming Paul for all this, we ought also to think about the scandal of one Catholic diocese (San Bernardino) proposing to sue another Catholic diocese (Boston) in civil court.

Maybe Paul was not entirely wrong in seeing such actions as sources of scandal.

Use Scripture as a Resource

The Bible is an important part of our religious heritage. Vatican II called Scripture "the soul of theology" and insisted that it permeate all our catechesis and worship. Of course, Catholics are not fundamentalists, and we are fully aware of the cultural gap between the first and the twenty-first centuries. Scripture does not have all the answers to our problems today. But Scripture can supply direction and consolation.

In academic circles, it has become a cliché to say that history is written by the winners. But that is not true of the Bible. Much of the Old Testament was put into the form that has come down to us only after the destruction of the Jerusalem Temple in 587 B.C. and the exile of Judah's leaders to Babylon. Out of these crises came the editing of the Torah (to provide a guide for God's people) and the narrative of Israel's history from Moses and Joshua to the exile (to remind the people of the negative effects of rebellion against the God of Israel). The collections of sayings from and about the great prophets—Isaiah, Jeremiah, and Ezekiel—took shape during the exile, and their calls for the renewal of God's people have echoed throughout the past 2500 years.

The current crisis in our Church has produced a great amount of suffering. The Old Testament lament psalms can provide the language in which to begin to express our pain and sorrow. These psalms also remind us that we constitute a community of sufferers, and give us freedom and permission to express our pain.

As we have seen throughout this paper, the New Testament, especially Paul's epistles, shows us that crisis and sin have been part of the Church's history, and that the paschal mystery can work forgiveness and reconciliation even in the midst of scandal. The epistles also remind us that, in earliest Christianity, unity rather than uniformity was the ideal, that the work of ministry was more important than titles and offices, and that women were significant contributors to the Pauline mission (see Romans 16:1-23). What gave unity to these diverse local communities was their common faith in the person of Jesus and the Pauline ideal of Christian life as "faith working through love" (Galatians 5:6). While Scripture may not have all the answers, it remains a precious resource in troubled times.

Promote Ongoing Formation in Christian Life

The current crisis has revealed dreadful shortcomings not only (but most obviously) in the seminary education of the past but also in the religious education and formation of the Catholic laity. Vatican II insisted that access to Scripture should be wide open to all the Christian faithful. But it is not enough to know that there are three parts to the Book of Isaiah and that Mark is the earliest gospel. Rather, we need to form people who live up to and incarnate the Pauline ideal of faith working through love.

The word "spirituality" is very popular today. The problem is that it can mean many different things. We need a Christian spirituality as profound and robust as what Paul presented in his Letter to the Romans. We need a Christian spirituality as wise and practical as what we find in the Book of Sirach and the Letter of James. We need a Christian spirituality as tested and humane as what emerges from struggling with the Book of Job and Mark's Gospel. We have wonderful spiritual resources in the Scriptures and elsewhere in our Catholic tradition, and we need to know and use them.

One promising bridge between Scripture and Christian life or spirituality is Christian virtue ethics. This approach to moral theology is less concerned with specific actions or with moral dilemmas as it is with three fundamental questions that pertain to human existence: Who am I? What is my end or goal in life? How do I get there?

In Christian virtue ethics, great attention is given to the paschal mystery and its effects. Among those effects are the three great theological virtues of faith, love, and hope. These virtues in turn give shape to the human virtues of prudence, justice, temperance, and fortitude, as well as to the more distinctive Christian virtues of fidelity, mercy or compassion, and humility. At the same time, there is awareness of the struggle against those vices that make our lives and the lives of others miserable and destructive. As Paul said in Galatians 5:22-23: "the fruit of the Spirit is love, joy, peace, patience, kindness, generosity, faithfulness, gentleness, and self-control. There is no law against such things." Behind this list is the Pauline ideal of faith working through love. This is what we need to cultivate in religious formation in these times of crisis in the Church.

2. What Can We Learn From the Church in the First Millennium?[1]

Rev. Michael J. Buckley, S.J., Boston College

Allow me to introduce these remarks by specifying briefly both the problematic situation out of which they arise and the question they attempt to address.[2]

(1) The problematic situation I should like to address in this chapter is not directly the horror and scandals of clerical sexual abuse, but what has emerged as its consequence: a crisis of confidence in the government of the Church, a crisis whose full dimensions remain to be assessed and whose character entails a far-reaching diminishment of the effective authority of the bishops and of the Holy See. We are dealing with a diminishment in credibility that is unparalleled, I believe, in the history of the Church in the United States.[3]

(2) Out of this situation comes the particular questions I have been asked to explore: What resources does the first millennium of

1. The following reflections were in formation for some time and delivered in part in Rome (December 1996) and as a unit initially at a panel discussion at Boston College (September 30, 2002) and then at a Conference in Kansas City (May 31, 2003). The Roman edition was published in *Il primato del successor e di Pietro: Atti del simposio teologico,Roma, dicembre 1996* (Vatican City: Liberia Editrice Vaticana, 1997) and in Michael J. Buckley, S.J., *Papal Primacy and the Episcopate. Towards a Relational Understanding* (New York: Crossroad Publishing Company, 1998). The lectures in Boston and Kansas City were recorded, and tapes from the latter meeting were distributed. After each of these presentations, the text was modified and augmented as suggestions and corrections were received and won agreement.

2. For this understanding of the problematic situation and the problem that is articulated as a question and gives some order and character to the indeterminate as a preparation for inquiry, see John Dewey, *Logic: The Theory of Inquiry* (New York: Holt, Rinehart and Winston, 1938), pp. 101-112.

3. See the Contemporary Catholic Trends poll conducted by LeMoyne College and Zogby International. "The number of American Catholics who think their bishops are doing a good job has fallen nearly 25 percentage points in the past eighteen months," from 81 percent in the fall of 2001 to 59 percent this spring. This rating is the "lowest in the poll's history." *The National Catholic Reporter,* May 23, 2003, p. 8.

the Church offer to address this crisis about leadership, especially as it involves the laity and the governance of the Church? What norms and practices of those centuries might we retrieve—however analogically—in order to redress the damage suffered by the Church in our time and to obviate its reoccurrence?

Obviously both these questions encompass a field far too vast and events far too intricate for a single response. But allow me— without naively canonizing the first thousand years of the Church (it was certainly no utopian society!)—to formulate four suggestions for consideration whose lineage derives from the convictions and normative practices of the first millennium. I emphasize the phrase "suggestions for consideration," because the following pages make a claim not to an apodictic assessment, but only to the judgment that these suggestions seem worth considering. Finally, the issue before the Church in the United States is not precisely to restore confidence in our time; that sounds too much like public relations. The issue is to have structures and the leadership in the Church that warrant this confidence.

~

My first suggestion: We must restore to the local church—and hence to the laity—a decisive voice in the selection of its own bishop.

"Decisive" can obviously mean many different things and be realized in many different ways, but in general it indicates that the selection of the local bishop should ordinarily be made by the local church and the regional bishops.[4] This was certainly the practice of the Church over much of its first millennium.

Some of the earliest documents of the Church number the

---

4. This would not, of course, rule out the papal veto in cases of genuine emergency or a papal intervention to guarantee the integrity of the process of selection. Of itself "a decisive voice" does not rule out other decisive voices. But what is at issue here is the usual government of the churches. Such a papal intervention could be understood not as an habitual, but as a substitutional use of primatial authority. For the "substitutional" use of papal authority in exceptional circumstances, see Michael J. Buckley, S.J., *Papal Primacy*, pp. 62-74.

election of bishops a grave and essential responsibility for all the members of the local church. The *Didache*, dating from the early second century, addresses all of those who participate in the Eucharist: "Therefore, elect/appoint [*cheirotonesate*] for yourselves bishops and deacons worthy of the Lord, meek men and not lovers of money, and truthful, for they also minister to you the ministry of the prophets and teachers."[5] In the third century, this responsibility dictated that three different groups collaborate in the selection of bishops: the laity of the local church, the clergy of the local church, and the bishops of that region, especially the metropolitan bishop. This was done in different manners, but all three components were present and vitally influential within an episcopal election.[6] *The Apostolic Tradition*, a work attributed to the redoubtable Hippolytus—the most prolific theological writer in Rome of the third century and both an antipope and a martyr!—insisted that the bishop is to be chosen *first* by *all* of the people [*hypo pantos tou laou*] and *then* that this initial election is to be approved subsequently by the assembled bishops and presbyters.[7] One can find a similar double election in the third century *Life of St. Polycarp.*[8] Cyprian, the magisterial third century African bishop and martyr, recognized the election of Cornelius as Bishop of Rome because he had been "made bishop by the judgment of God and of His Christ, by the testimony of almost all of the clergy, by the vote of the people who

---

5. *The Didache,* or *Teaching of the Twelve Apostles,* in *The Apostolic Fathers,* ed. with trans. Kirsopp Lake, Loeb Classical Library (London: William Heinemann, 1930), 15.1. Ferguson explains the term, *cheirotonesate,* in terms of its historical usage in Greece of the first and second century: "Magistrates in Greece were elected by the citizens. The vote was taken by a show of hands, which was the original meaning of *cheirotonia*" (Everett Ferguson, ed., *Encyclopedia of Early Christianity,* 2d ed. [New York: Garland Publishing, 1997], s.v. "Election to Church Office," by Everett Ferguson).

6. Buckley, *Papal Primacy,* p. 86.

7. Hippolytus of Rome, *The Treatise on the Apostolic Tradition,* eds. Gregory Dix and Henry Chadwick, 2d rev. ed. (London: Alba Press, 1992), 2:1-2, 2-3 (emphasis added).

8. See Hippolytus, *On the Apostolic Tradition,* an English version with introduction and commentary by Alistair Stewart-Sykes (Crestwood, New York: St. Vladimir's Seminary Press, 2001), pp. 56-57.

were then present, by the college of venerable bishops and good men...."⁹ This combination was crucial for Cyprian, for "he stated emphatically that the *entire community—clergy, laity, and neighboring bishops*—should participate in the selection of episcopal leaders."¹⁰ In the same period, Origen, possibly the greatest theologian of that century in the Church, insisted that "the presence of the laity was essential in episcopal elections."¹¹ An imperial variation in this process was recorded by the ecclesiastical historian Sozomen, writing of the appointment of John Chrysostom at the end of the fourth century to the See of Constantinople: "John was adjudged worthy, in word and in deed, by all the subjects of the Roman empire, to preside over the Church of Constantinople. The clergy and people were unanimous in electing him; *their choice* was approved by the emperor; messengers were dispatched for John."¹²

The shifting of the popular suffrage to an acclamation or a rejection by the laity of the choice of the local priests or bishops seems to have evolved over the centuries that followed in that millennium and found its spare articulation in the *Decretum* of Gratian in the eleventh century: "Election belongs to clerics; consent [to this

---

9. Thascius Caecilius Cyprianus, *Epistulae*, in vol. 3, pt. 2 of *Corpus Scriptorum Ecclesiasticorum Latinorum*, ed. W. Von Hartel (Vienna, 1871), Letter 55.8; the English translation used here is Saint Cyprian, *Letters (1-81)*, trans. Sister Rose Bernard Donna, *The Fathers of the Church*, vol. 51 (Washington, D.C.: The Catholic University of America Press, 1964), p. 138. See W. H. C. Frend, *The Rise of Christianity* (Philadelphia: Fortress Press, 1984), p. 403.

10. Patrick Granfield, "Episcopal Elections in Cyprian: Clerical and Lay Participation," *Theological Studies* 37 (1996), p. 41; emphasis added.

11. Frend, *The Rise of Christianity*, 428 n. 39. Frend is reporting the judgment of Origen as in Origen, *Homily on Leviticus*, ed. W. A. Baehrens, *Die griechichen christlihen Scriftsteller der ersten drei Jahrhunderten*, Origen (Leipzig: Hinrichs, 1920), III. 20.

12. Sozomen, *The Ecclesiastical History of Sozomen, Comprising a History of the Church from A.D. 324 to A.D. 440*, trans. Edward Walford (London: Henry G. Bohn, 1855), bk. 8, ch. 2, p. 364; emphasis added.

13. Robert L. Benson, *The Bishop-Elect: A Study in Medieval Ecclesiastical Office* (Princeton: Princeton University Press, 1968), 33. One finds vestiges of this need for the consent of the people in the address of the bishop to the people during the Ordination of Priests in

election], to the people."[13] But in the centuries before Gratian, this acclamation of the laity had exercised a "constitutive power."[14] One must not exaggerate the regularity over these centuries nor discount the problems of civil unrest, rivalries, factions, and ambition that this mode of episcopal selection sometimes unleashed, as Augustine recorded.[15] Also, the chaos of history played out as the lines of development afforded increased power to the local clergy. But despite the heightened clericalization of the process, it is important to underline that the local church, and here, the laity together with the local clergy and bishops in the first millennium had—or was expected to have—in one way or another, a decisive voice in the selection of its bishops.

Nor was this simply a usage into which the Church fell. On the contrary, this universal practice was founded on a principle taught and stated starkly by Pope Leo the Great in the fifth century: "Let the one who is going to rule over all be elected by all [*qui praefuturus est omnibus, ab omnibus eligatur*]." Leo concretized this maxim, as Robert L. Benson notes, by insisting that a "proper election needs not only the will of the clergy, but also of the more eminent laymen

---

the previous *Pontificale Romanum*: "Not without cause did the Fathers direct that the people should also be consulted in the choice of those who are to minister at the altar. For sometimes what is unknown to the many of the life and conduct of a candidate may be known to the few, and a more ready obedience is given to a priest when assent has been given to his ordination. Now the conduct of these deacons, whom by God's help we are about to ordain priests, has been tried and found (as far as I can judge) pleasing to God, and deserving, in my opinion, of a higher ecclesiastical dignity. But as the judgment of one person, or even of several, may perhaps be mistaken or led astray by partiality, it is well to ascertain the general opinion." "The Ordination of Priests," *The Rites of Ordination and Episcopal Consecration*, with English Translation approved by the National Conference of Catholic Bishops of the United States of America and Confirmed by the Apostolic See (Washington, D.C.: National Conference of Catholic Bishops, 1967), p. 34. The revised "Rite of Ordination" omits this exhortation, the *ordinandi* being presented to the bishop with the assurance that the people of God have been consulted in the past.

14. Benson, *Bishop-Elect*, p. 36.

15. See Henry Chadwick, *The Church in Ancient Society. From Galilee to Gregory the Great* (Oxford: Oxford University Press, 2001), p. 314.

and of the common people."[16] But this fifth century papal maxim did little more than render in lapidary form what Pope Celestine I had stipulated more than a century before: "A bishop should not be given to those who are unwilling [to receive him]. The consent and the wishes of the clergy, the people, and the nobility are required."[17] Note that it is the Roman See—not simply some provincial church— that is insisting so strongly on the freedom of the local church to elect its own bishop. Benson states that this dictum of Celestine I underlay the electoral theory throughout the Early Middle Ages. Even the preference of the bishops of the province was not of itself deci- sive. The laity and the local clergy had to be consulted.[18] For centu- ries, the Roman See saw its primatial powers as a support of the freedom of the local church in times of great crisis. As late as the Council of Rheims (1049)—the end of the first millennium—pre- sided over by Pope Leo IX, this Gregorian formula appeared and was to reappear again and again in the centuries that followed: "the bishop had to be 'chosen by the clergy and the people.' "[19] Even in the great lay investiture struggles between Gregory VII and Henry IV in the next millennium (eleventh century), the effort of the papacy was not to transfer power from the secular lords to the Apostolic See but "to win the freedom of the local church in selecting their bishops."[20]

---

16. Benson, *Bishop-Elect*, p. 25. Benson is citing this dictum of Leo, which has remark- able similarities to a statement of Pliny the Younger, from *Ep.* 10, c.6. PL 54:634. See Benson for similar assertions of the election of the bishop by all concerned and the application in the Early and Medieval Church of the principle of Roman law: "quod omnibus similiter tangit, ab omnibus comprobetur."

17. Ibid. Benson is citing this dictum of Celestine from *Ep.* 4, c.5, PL 50:434: "Nullus invitis detur episcopus. Cleri, plebis et ordinis consensus ac desiderium requiratur."

18. Ibid, pp. 24-25.

19. See Jean Gaudemet, "The Choice of Bishops; A Tortuous History," in *From Law to Life*, eds. James Provost and Knut Walf, Concilium 1996/5 (London: SCM Press, 1996), pp. 60-61.

20. William Henn, O.F.M. Cap., "Historical-Theological Synthesis of the Relation Be- tween Primacy and Episcopacy During the Second Millennium," *Il primato del successore de Pietro: atti del simposio teologico, Roma, dicembre 1996* (Vatican City: Libreria Editrice Vaticana, 1997), p. 225.

Now, let me explain why I give this particular retrieval of the past pride of place. Very simply, I think we would get better bishops in greater numbers. I do not mean this as an anti-episcopal jab. My experience with the American bishops convinces me that so very many of them are deeply dedicated men, doggedly attempting to meet the responsibilities of their office in a very difficult time. The Church in the United States has much to admire among its bishops, but I think that the Church can do still better, and, in some cases, much better. I think that the committed Catholic laity and the clergy of a locale—working possibly through a diocesan pastoral council and priest senate—would obviously be in a position to judge both the serious needs of the diocese and the religious capacities of the candidates, especially for religious leadership, far better than a papal nuncio under the influence of those he has chosen to consult.

It is simply scandalous to hear, in diocese after diocese, the local clergy voice their fears about who will be imposed upon them because he is well connected in Rome or recommended by a restorationalist theology. It is scandalous to listen to their aching discouragement that so-and-so has been appointed bishop of their diocese because of his close identification with powerful ecclesiastical figures that he has assiduously cultivated over the years. "Testimony from all over the world," wrote Archbishop Quinn some four years ago, "points to a widespread dissatisfaction with the present procedure for the appointment of bishops."[21] James O'Toole, the distinguished historian of the Church in Boston, cites precisely these contemporary procedures for the selection of a bishop as bringing about the scandals and political struggles for power that have ridden the Church in Boston: "At the heart of the problem was the procedure by which Catholic bishops were chosen during the O'Connell Century [i.e., the 20th century]."[22]

---

21. John R. Quinn, *The Reform of the Papacy: The Costly Call to Christian Unity* (New York: Crossroad Publishing Company, 1999), p. 133.

22. James O'Toole, "A Cardinal's Coverup," *The Boston Globe Online*, 12 January 2003, <http://www.boston.com/dailyglobe2/012/focus/A_cardinal_s_coverup+.shtml>(13 January 2003).2

Professor O'Toole finds the present procedures for the selection of bishops hopelessly compromised because "ambitious prelates could lobby advancement and succeed, because they only needed to persuade a handful of officials in Rome to obtain the prize."[23] He recalls O'Connell's "actively campaigning for promotion to Boston, funneling large contribution to various Vatican causes and loudly protesting that he was more loyal to the papacy than anyone else...." And O'Toole added: "Others followed his example."[24] John Quinn criticizes this procedure for its "choosing candidates who can be trusted to be safe....But the problem is that 'orthodoxy' can be confused with integralism. Integralism may be described as a kind of narrowness and intolerance, raising private opinions and viewpoints to the level of dogma."[25]

It is not simply the present crisis in the United States that has raised the question of the adequacy of this protocol of episcopal selection. One hears the same growing alienation in country after country throughout the world, as Archbishop Quinn has stated. One is reminded of the statement of Augustine that was so crucially important in the life of John Henry Newman: "*Securus judicat orbis terrarum*" (The judgment of the entire world is certain).[26] The Church must find its way back to a better way of selecting and appointing bishops, and it is here—it seems to me—that the normative practices of the Church in its first millennium offer some very promising suggestions.

---

23. Ibid.

24. Ibid.

25. Quinn, *Reform of the Papacy*, pp. 134-135. The Archbishop continues: "[But] it should be possible to find candidates who are not only orthodox in the true sense, but who are also endowed with critical judgment, imagination, and who are open to new ideas. Fidelity to the mission of the Church requires candidates who can listen, listen to the world, listen to the people, and who have the spiritual discernment and critical judgment to endorse what is good, reject what is evil, and not stifle the Spirit" (135).

26. Augustine, *Contra epist. Parmen,* III. 24. PL 43, 101. For Newman's reception of this maxim, see John Henry Newman, *Apologia pro vita sua, Being a History of His Religious Opinions,* ed. Martin J. Svaglic (Oxford: Clarendon Press, 1967) Ch. 3: 109-111.

One should obviously not become rhapsodic about a retrieval of something like this earlier protocol of the first millennium. Those centuries sometimes saw great problems in attempts at political control, manipulation, and civic disturbance in the selection of a bishop. The Church would have to learn from that history and these dangers would have to be provided for as is done in the selection of a college president, a superior of a religious community, an administrator of a major health facility, or a Benedictine abbot. There are many different ways in which the local church could be given substantive electoral responsibility and work out in practice a decisive voice in the selection of its bishop. They need not be the same; each would have to be adapted to the culture of the locale. There is nothing in the first thousand years of the history of the Church to suggest that the primacy of the Roman See should entitle or require its occupant to determine who is to be the bishop of every see in the Church. There may have been many good reasons that have led to this present settlement as the Church struggled successively for its freedom from the political control and the hegemony of the absolute state. But one must recognize that—in much of the world—those days are, for the most part, gone, and that the Church would profit immensely from retrieving something of the freedom and self-direction of the local churches of the first millennium. I fear it is necessary to state this more emphatically: if the present system for the selection of bishops is not redressed, all other attempts at serious reform will founder and ever greater numbers of Catholics will move towards alienation, disinterest, and affective schism. I believe that the situation is that serious.

~

The second suggestion I submit for consideration is this: the Church should restore the *enduring* commitment of the bishop to his see.

The Church should reaffirm again, strongly and effectively, the ancient canonical prohibition, forbidding a bishop's leaving one see to obtain another. The fifteenth canon of the Council of Nicea, the fifth canon of Chalcedon, and many regional councils insistently enjoined bishops—or priests and deacons—from moving from one see to another. The bishop was considered bound to his people by a mystical union that was "expressed as being akin to the marriage bond." Thus the Council of Alexandria (338) went so far as to call a bishop who had moved from one see to another an adulterer.[27] Translations from one see to another did occur in the first millennium, but it required something like a claim of divine revelation or an action by an episcopal synod to justify it in terms of the urgent needs of another church, and even then, as Hamilton Hess has remarked, "we find that nearly all proposed and effected translations were regarded with a degree of suspicion."[28] The Church in the West was far stricter in this matter than in the East. Paradoxically perhaps, no see in the first millennium was more faithful to these canonical prohibitions than Rome itself. The Roman Church never elected a bishop from another see to become bishop of Rome until late in the ninth century (882), with Marinus I, originally bishop of Caere (Certvetri), whose pontificate was followed by the horrors of the papacy at the end of the ninth century and most of the tenth.[29]

Why such an insistence? Because the early Church saw quite practically in this effort to move from one see to another an endless source of clerical ambition, rivalry, and self-promotion, as well as, more theologically, the violation of the union that should exist between the bishop and the people of his diocese. Sarcastically, the first canon of the Council of Sardica (342) noted: "Almost no bishop is found who will move from a large city to a small one…whence it appears that they are inflamed by the heat of avarice to serve ambition."[30]

These concerns of the Church for centuries were not simply silly. Ambition and its correlative fears can tempt to a time-serving

---

27. Hamilton Hess, *The Canons of the Council of Sardica, A.D. 343* (Oxford; Clarendon Press, 1958), pp. 71-75. See Buckley, *Papal Primacy*, pp. 90-92

28. Ibid, p. 73.

29. See Buckley, *Papal Primacy*, p. 93.

30. Hess, *Sardica*, pp. 76-77.

careerism in which one adjusts his statements and positions in order to cultivate a higher authority who can advance his career from one see to a greater one. This would have been impossible in much of the first millennium. This is not to condemn those who quite legitimately have followed the protocols of our own time. If one looks at the major sees in the United States, very many of their bishops have advanced from lesser dioceses to greater. But I think, finally, that the normative usages of an early time were much better.

For one cannot but ask honestly whether the contemporary system does not effectively turn these lesser sees into farm teams to prepare men for the big leagues, rather than a holy people in whom the bishop had—in a sacred and irrefragable bond—invested his life permanently. This procedure denigrates the sacred importance of the diocese if it is small, encourages regressive ambitions and even competition within the episcopate, and seriously damages the bishop's effective and affective union with the local presbyterate and laity—a union that it takes years to develop.

It is heartening to note that voices in the Holy See, such as those of Cardinal Gantin and Cardinal Ratzinger, have so strongly and so recently condemned this translation from one see to another. In May of 1999, Cardinal Gantin, Prefect Emeritus of the Congregation of Bishops and then Dean of the College of Cardinals, spoke of the need to restore the ancient canonical prohibitions against the advancement of bishop from see to see in order to eliminate, he said, "social climbing and 'careerism.'" His remarks occasioned, as you might expect, strong protest from some, Cardinal Ruini among them, but they evoked an even stronger agreement from Cardinal Ratzinger the following month: "I totally agree with Cardinal Gantin. In the Church, above all, there should be no sense of careerism....There can be exceptional cases...a very large See where experience of episcopal ministry is necessary, *could* be an exception. But it should not be common practice; it should happen only in the *most exceptional cases.*"[31]

---

31. The interviews with Cardinals Gantin and Ratzinger were reported in *Trenti giourni* and delivered to the press in the United States by ZENIT International Agency. See

My first suggestion, then, urges that the local church, clerics and laity, should have a critically determinative voice in the selection of its bishop. The second suggestion urges the restoration of the permanent, mutual commitment of the bishop to his clergy and to his people until the bishop leaves the active ministry. Both of these were normative in the first millennium. Their retrieval is suggested here in order to counter problematic settlements in the contemporary Church that most Christians of the first millennium would have considered illegitimate and corrupting.

~

My third suggestion: The Church needs to restore or strengthen episcopal conferences and regional gatherings of local bishops.

The history of the first centuries of the Church bears witness to innumerable regional gatherings of the bishops of local churches in Asia, Africa, and Spain. This was simply how the Church was governed. "Over four hundred synods and meetings of bishops, Eastern and Western, [are] known to have been held between the mid-second century and the pontificate of Gregory the Great....Most were local or provincial gatherings, others included all the bishops of a larger political region or 'diocese.'"[32] They could and did legislate with a majority—ideally a consensus—constituting their collective judgment. The purpose of these local meetings was multiple, but all of them bore upon the responsibility of the region to settle its own serious problems, whether of doctrine or of order or of discipline. There is an amusing remark by the pagan historian Ammianus Marcellinus that "the public transportation system, during the reign of Constantius II [337-61] was paralyzed by Christian bishops traveling to and from their [numerous] synods at the

---

"Bishops Divided Between Diocesan Fidelity and 'Careerism,'" *The Daily Catholic,* 21 July 1999, <http://dailycatholic.org/issue/archives/1999Jul/135jul21,vol.10, no.135txt/jul21dc2.htm> (15 January 2003); emphasis added.

32. Brian Daley, "Structures of Charity: Bishops' Gathering and the See of Rome in the Early Church," in *Episcopal Conferences: Historical, Canonical and Theological Studies,* ed. Thomas J. Reese, S.J. (Washington, D.C.: Georgetown University Press, 1989), p. 28.

imperial expense."[33] But by means of these regional meetings, the local churches could and did govern themselves. If massive and intractable internal contradictions occurred, then the issue could be referred to the Apostolic See. But this relatively rare practice itself was susceptible of great variety. The historical situation was very complex, but by and large, Rome did not interfere in the life of the churches in Africa, Asia, and Spain or attempt to govern them. On the contrary, it often acted to protect the integrity and freedom of the local Church. It was Julius I who intervened to protest the deposition of Athanasius from the See of Alexandria. It was Innocent I who came to the defense of John Chrysostom in Constantinople.[34] Nicea had legislated that the local bishops were to gather twice a year, and "the efforts of the popes—especially those with a strong sense of universal leadership like Leo and Gregory—were often directed towards encouraging bishops to observe the canonical requirement of regular provincial and regional meetings."[35] As mentioned previously, even the massive claims of Gregory VII were introduced to safeguard the freedom of the local churches.

The contrast with the present situation of the Church could hardly be greater. I think it is fair to say that the Church has never been so centralized as it has become today, a centralization abetted by the modern means of communication. International synods of bishops are fixed at little more than consultative meetings, advising the pope in his government—not *their* government—of the Church and awaiting the definitive action of the Holy See. There is widespread belief that even the agenda is carefully controlled by the Roman Curia. Local episcopal conferences have been crippled in their practices and deprived of much of their authority by the most recent provisions set by the Holy See. To pass something as a teaching

---

See Christopher O'Donnell, *Ecclesia: A Theological Encyclopedia of the Church* (Collegeville, Minn.: The Liturgical Press, 1996), s.v. "Councils."

33. Daley, "Bishops' Gatherings," pp. 28-29.

34. Ibid., pp. 41-42.

35. Ibid., p. 45.

act of the conference, the Holy See has imposed upon these conferences as a necessary condition a unanimity of judgment that no
synod or provincial council ever had to meet in the first millennium—or even now. Failing this, the decision must now be referred
to the determination of the Holy See. The Curia's treatment of the
International Commission on English in the Liturgy has been cited by
Bishops Trautman and Maurice Taylor as scandalous, while virtually
unanimous judgments of national hierarchies have been set aside by
Roman congregations acting with the authority of the pope.[36]

Almost everything in the Church is ruled finally by Roman pre-
scriptions or Roman officials, despite the increasing anger that this
denial of local authority is awakening. There is a growing restive-
ness in the Church in the United States that is unprecedented. And I
wonder if very neuralgic and delicate issues such as presently divide
the Church would not have been handled more successfully if they
had made their way through open, careful conversations among

---

36. One thinks, for example, of the treatment meted out to the National Conference's
decision regarding the implementation of *Ex corde ecclesiae* and the decision on the age
of confirmation. In 1982, the US Bishops voted to permit a trial use of the Common
Lectionary on a limited basis; the Congregation for Divine Worship and the Discipline
of the Sacraments [CDWDS] denied the *confirmatio* of the bishops' decision the following year. Around 1993, the American bishops voted three separate acts of approval and
submitted them to Rome for *confirmatio*: (1) the revised Lectionary based on the NAB,
especially the revised NAB New Testament; (2) the liturgical use of the revised NAB
psalter; (3) the use of the NRSV Lectionary. The Congregation denied absolutely the
decisions on the revised NAB psalter (largely for inclusive language reasons) and also
denied the NRSV Lectionary, saying each conference should have only one Scripture
translation for use in the liturgy. Rome also denied *confirmatio* of the NAB Lectionary
and asked the Bishops' Conference to send representatives to Rome to discuss the matter. In Sept 1997, the CDWDS denied its approval or confirmation of the proposed ICEL
Ordination Rites approved by the USCCB. In March 2002, the same Congregation refused its approval or confirmation of the proposed ICEL translation of the Second Edition of the Roman Missal, despite the fact that it had been approved not only by the US
Conference of Bishops but by nine other conferences as well. The content or justification of each of these various reversals is not in question here; what is at issue is that an
episcopal conference can be so frequently overridden by curial action, as if the bishops
were incompetent to decide about the pastoral needs of their people, the translation of
the Scriptures into their own language, and the conduct of liturgy within their diocese
or national conference.

regional gatherings of bishops—as was done in the early Church—before being considered by the Holy See. In such local and regional gatherings, the voice, the experience, and the concerns of the laity have a much greater chance of an effective presence.

That Rome should encourage and support strong regional and national episcopal conferences, which would incorporate the experience of the members of the local churches, would not set a course contrary to the primacy of Roman See. On the contrary, it would realize much of the fraternal ministry of the primacy, the strengthening and unification of the bishops that Vatican I in *Pastor aeternus* gave as the purpose of the primacy.[37]

~

My fourth and final suggestion: To counter the present excessive centralization within the Church, certain institutions that may at one time have served a useful purpose, need to be reconsidered and perhaps even abolished.

They were either entirely absent from the first millennium or far more modest in their presence. I think of such institutions, for example, as the college of cardinals, the office of papal nuncio, the appointment as "bishops" in the Roman Curia of those who have no local church they administer, and even such honorific attachments to the papal court as "monsignor."

Theologically or sacramentally, the "sacred college" is not the college of cardinals, but the college of bishops. The origins of the

---

37. See Vatican I, Fourth Session, *Pastor aeternus*, the First Dogmatic Constitution on the Church of Christ, July 18, 1870, DS 3061: "This power of the Supreme Pontiff is far from standing in the way of the power of ordinary and immediate episcopal jurisdiction by which the bishops who, under appointment of the Holy Spirit (see Acts 20:28), succeeded in the place of the apostles, feed and rule individually, as true shepherds, the particular flock assigned to them. Rather this latter power is *asserted, confirmed and vindicated by this same supreme and universal shepherd*, as in the words of St. Gregory the Great: 'My honor is the honor of the whole Church. My honor is the firm strength of my brothers. I am truly honored when due honor is paid to each and everyone.'" ET: *The Christian Faith: In the Doctrinal Documents of the Catholic Church*, eds. J. Neuner and J. Dupuis (New York: Alba, 1982); emphasis added; see also Ibid. DS 3050-3051.

college of cardinals are "obscure," but for all of its variations it be-speaks four functions within the Roman Church: to advise the pope, to elect the pope, to execute various papal offices, and to govern the Church when there is no pope. But *de facto* cardinals are given pre-cedence even over bishops and patriarchs, whose function is not primarily to advise the pope but to govern and lead the Church with the pope.[38] It might make better ecclesial sense—especially with the growing international position of the papacy—to have the pope elected in some way by the Church at Rome and by representatives of various episcopal conferences. The present settlement—that the cardinalate provides for election of the pope by the Church of Rome—seems little more than a legal fiction.

One wonders further if the papal nuncio is a novelty that should be reconsidered, a permanent representative of the Apos-tolic See or ambassador to a secular government. It makes a good deal of sense to have an apostolic delegate represent the Holy Father to the Church in the United States, but the representation of the Church in the United States to the American body politic should be through its bishops and its own officials. What is sac-ramentally important is that the college of bishops—with the pope as its head and in vital, effective contact with the people who constitute the Church—actually govern and represent the Church.

A Final Word

These are the four suggestions I submit for consideration about the Church that is still very young. It is only two thousand years old—still growing and sent into a world that will last for many more thousands of centuries. There is nothing in these suggestions

---

38. O'Donnell, *Ecclesia*, s.v. "Cardinals." Cardinals rank only after the pope in hierarchy: "Since the twelfth century, the cardinals have had precedence over archbishops and bish-ops, and since the fifteenth century, even over patriarchs (bull: *Non mediocri* of Pope Eugene IV, 1431-47)." Salvador Miranda, "Cardinal" in the *New Catholic Encyclopedia*, 2nd edition (Detroit: Gale, 2002), 3:105. In the secret consistory of June 10, 1630, Urban VIII granted to the cardinals the title of "eminence."

that a very ordinary theology of the Church could not sanction, but one must recognize that to effect anything like these suggestions, the primatial leadership of the pope would be of critical importance.

The only single influence now that could lead the Church to the restorations of the structures, to the freedoms and the self-direction the individual churches enjoyed in the first millennium, is papal. Even conciliar leadership would be dependent upon that initiative or confirmation. These four suggestions that the first thousand years could offer to the present crisis are both ordinary and radical. They are ordinary in the sense that for this period many of them were normative practices, followed in usage and taught in theory throughout the Church; radical, for they indicate a correction, even a reversal, to the excessive centralization of present Church governance. If these suggestions are found to be sound, still only the pope, exercising his primacy with and within the college of bishops, would have both the ecclesial credibility and the international position to restore—possibly working with another ecumenical council—to the local and regional churches what was once unquestionably theirs and what seems so needed now to address the present crisis in leadership.

It was precisely the structures of the first millennium that John Paul II praised so strongly in *Ut unum sint* and urged as a guide to the present Church in its dealing with the Orthodox: "The structures of the Church in the East and in the West evolved in reference to that Apostolic heritage. Her unity during the first millennium was maintained within those same structures through the Bishops, Successors of the Apostles, in communion with the Bishop of Rome. If today at the end of the second millennium we are seeking to restore full communion, it is to that unity, *thus structured*, which we must look."[39] And even more strongly: "The structures of unity which existed before the separation are a heritage of experience that guides our common path towards the re-establishment of full

---

39. John Paul II, *Ut unum sint* (May 25, 1995), 55; emphasis added.

communion."[40] It is precisely those structures of the first millennium that gave the local Church and its laity far greater and effective presence in its government.

In that same remarkable encyclical, the pope recognized his responsibility "to find a way of exercising the primacy which, while in
no way renouncing what is essential to its mission, is none the less
open to a new situation." He asked that the pastors and theologians
of the Church would seek for contemporary "forms in which this
[papal] ministry may accomplish a service of love recognized by all
concerned."[41] One wonders if leadership in the retrieval of these
forms and structures, which have been suggested above and by which
the local church existed in the first millennium, could not be part of
that papal ministry.

It may seem to some that these four suggestions evince restless
discontent. That is not the case. They hold in great reverence the
Church as the people of God and as the body of Christ. As this, they
experience it as holy—whatever its history also of sins, defects, and
failures. But it is this very demanding vocation to holiness that dic-
tates the need for continual self-examination and reform. And to
meet that need, I think we have much to learn from our first thousand years.

---

40. Ibid., 56.

41. Ibid., 95. In this request to pastors and theologians of the Church, the encyclical is
citing from the homily of John Paul II in the presence of the Ecumenical Patriarch,
Dimitrios I (6 December 1987), 3; *AAS* 80 (1988), 714.

3. What Can We Learn From the Medieval Church?

Dr. Catherine M. Mooney, Weston Jesuit School of Theology

Ecclesia semper reformanda est: The Church is always in need of reform. As an imperfect institution striving always for perfection, we should be neither surprised nor scandalized to acknowledge that the Church needs to be reformed. Indeed, since its very inception, the Church has regularly engaged in explicit efforts to reform itself. In this essay, I will discuss four such instances of Church reform during the period A.D. 1000 to 1600, and suggest how each raises relevant points for contemporary discussions of Church reform. Specifically, these reforms show that medieval practices, theologies, and experiences of being Church, far from buttressing today's highly top-down, monarchical mode of church governance, provide historical precedents and arguments for a more inclusive and representative model of Church.

The first reform movement, the Gregorian reform, highlights a battle among the elites of medieval society—popes, prelates, emperors, kings, and powerful lay lords—about the role of the laity in the selection of bishops. The second reform foregrounds an unprecedented evangelical awakening in which laywomen and men asserted their own religious authority and the hierarchical church responded. The third reform movement, the conciliar movement, illustrates how a severe church crisis spawned a movement to replace the papacy's monarchical mode of governance with a constitutional model of church polity. A final instance of reform is drawn from the Council of Trent, and takes up the issue of the role of the bishop within the Church.

The Gregorian Reform: Lay Involvement in Church Appointments

The Gregorian reform, named after the eleventh-century Pope Gregory VII, denotes a sweeping reform movement that extended from about the year 1050 to the year 1300 and which, broadly conceived, aimed to delineate the proper spheres of action for religious and secular authorities. I will focus on just one of the reform's specific goals: the attempt to eliminate the involvement of laymen in the selection of abbots, bishops, and even the pope. Although this reform focuses particularly on socially powerful laymen, it highlights some pivotal issues regarding the role of the laity in general within the Church.

There is a long history of lay involvement in the selection of bishops. Since Emperor Constantine's conversion in the fourth century, ties joining the Church and secular rule had grown progressively more involved. On the one hand, churchmen exercised authority in secular affairs, and on the other, secular rulers exercised authority in religious affairs. With the gradual disintegration of Roman rule, for example, bishops, including the bishop of Rome, in a spontaneous and naturally logical move, assumed ever-widening secular responsibilities within their societies. They helped to keep the order, settle disputes, make laws, and provide social services. In violent and chaotic times, bishops even raised and led armies. Throughout the Middle Ages, moreover, it was commonly (and mistakenly) believed that Constantine had granted to Pope Silvester (314-35) and his successors secular power over the lands of the western Roman Empire.[1] Popes and bishops acting as civil authorities flies in the face of our modern notions regarding the separation of church and state, but prior to the year 1000, people failed to discern clear lines demarcating spiritual and temporal governance. Church and state, as two entirely discrete entities, simply did not exist.

Similarly, secular rulers exercised religious authority. It was commonly assumed by everyone in the Middle Ages that kings received

---

1. Constantine allegedly made this grant to Silvester and his successors after Silvester supposedly cured Constantine's leprosy and taught him the faith. The *Donation of Constantine*, widely thought to be a decree issued in 317, was in fact a forgery composed probably by a papal cleric in the mid-eighth century. Although suspected by some people to be a fake, it was definitively shown to be false only in the mid-fourteenth century by Lorenzo de Valla.

their authority directly from God. As such, a good king was not simply a secular authority; he was also the protector of the Church and promoter of Christian belief. Ruler and pope alike were ordained by God to rule; and, in varying degrees, both had spiritual and temporal responsibilities. A case in point is the Frankish king Charlemagne (742-814), often called both *rex* [king] and *sacerdos* [priest].[2] He was crowned as Holy Roman Emperor by Pope Leo III (795-816) on Christmas day, 800. Charlemagne enthusiastically promoted ecclesiastical reforms, orthodox belief, and the conversion of Saxons and Slavs. He incorporated canon laws, that is, church laws, into his own legislation to regulate such things as excommunication, the qualifications and duties of bishops, how priests should be educated, and how they should behave in public. He laid down numerous pastoral directives: he decreed that priests were to teach the Lord's Prayer, explain the Trinity, and preach about love of God and neighbor. On Sundays, he commanded the laity to rest from work and attend Mass. They were to acknowledge their sins, forgive others, and help the poor.[3] Not the ideal ruler in every respect, Charlemagne nonetheless used his position to promote Christianity in his realm.

For good or ill, he and other feudal rulers also exercised significant control over local churches. They built churches for the peasants and villagers inhabiting their lands and staffed them with priests. A priest's income would often be generated by peasants working the land around the church, land granted by the lord to support the priest and his church. At a higher level of secular rule, kings, emperors, and even lay lords quite frequently played the same role vis-à-vis bishops: they chose and appointed the bishops, often in consultation with other bishops they had appointed, and they endowed

---

2. R.W. Southern, "The Church of the Dark Ages, 600-1000," p. 95, in *The Layman in Christian History*, eds. Stephen Charles Neill and Hans-Ruedi Weber (London: SCM Press, 1963). The term "priest" was applied to Charlemagne and other Frankish rulers with regard to their leadership roles in religious disputes and theological problems. It did not suggest they could administer the sacraments.

3. Rosamund McKitterick, *The Frankish Church and the Carolingian Reforms, 789-895* (London: Royal Historical Society, 1977).

the bishops' churches with vast income-generating lands. Historians have designated this the era of the "proprietary church"—*proprietary* because in a very real sense, the Church, and the churches it comprised, was owned by the emperor, kings, and local lay rulers. And perhaps it will surprise no one that it was not always spiritual concerns that motivated kings in their desire to control episcopal appointments. Indeed, bishops were comparable to dukes or counts. They might be the sole secular authority in a town or rural area. Kings counted on them as they would any lay lord to keep the order, to marshal armies, and even to fight, themselves, on occasion. Rulers often preferred bishops and abbots to lay counts because men who were celibate in theory, and often in fact, would not attempt to convert the lands they used into a hereditary right.

The very idea of the laity having significant roles in the appointment of bishops will strike the modern Catholic as bizarre. In fact, the manner of electing bishops has changed over time. During the first thousand years of the Church, it involved both the local laity and clergy, the very people who would be familiar with the candidate and know their own needs. Pope Leo the Great (440-61), reflecting early church practice, was simply stating the obvious when he wrote, "He who is to be in charge of all should be chosen by all." More specifically, he stated, "The approval of the clergy, the testimony of those of noble rank, and the agreement of the common people should be had."[4] Scholarly studies of this time show that the "agreement" or "consent" of the people involved their active participation in the selection process.[5] Early medieval church councils in

---

4. Letter 10, in Leo the Great, *Letters*, trans. Edmund Hunt (New York: Fathers of the Church, 1957), p. 44.

5. Thomas F. O'Meara, "Emergence and Decline of Popular Voice in the Selection of Bishops," in *The Choosing of Bishops* (Hartford, CT: Canon Law Society of America, 1971), pp. 23-32; Anscar Parsons, *Canonical Elections: An Historical Synopsis and Commentary* (Washington, D.C.: Catholic University of America Press, 1939), pp. 23-26; John Albert Eidenschink, *The Election of Bishops in the Letters of Gregory the Great* (Washington, D.C.: Catholic University of America Press, 1945), pp. 80-85; Peter Stockmeier, "The Election of Bishops by Clergy and People in the Early Church," in *Electing Our Own Bishops*, eds. Peter Huizing and Knut Walf (New York: Seabury Press, 1980), pp. 3-9.

Gaul decreed that bishops were to be elected by the clergy and laity of a vacant see, and then consecrated by the metropolitan, the principal bishop of a region.

By the seventh century, with the advent of feudal modes of governing in a decidedly more chaotic world, the laity involved in the selection of bishops were powerful lay lords. Until at least the year 1000, it was common for them to be influential, indeed, often decisive, in the selection of bishops and abbots. Canon law required that the actual *election* of bishops reside in the hands of the clergy, but in fact lay lords easily won ratification of their choices by abbots, senior clergy, and the other bishops in their realms.

The pope had nothing to do with episcopal elections in dioceses beyond the vicinity of Rome and was himself sometimes put into office by laymen. In only rare cases was a disputed election sent to him for consideration. Even in these cases, the pope did not himself make the appointment, and it was possible that his opinion be ignored.[6] In the tenth century, popes were put into office not by the clergy (which is what canon law required), but by whomever happened to control Rome—either the German kings and emperors or a noble Roman family. An often ignored fact is that the German emperors generally made good appointments to the papacy, while the Roman nobility usually made bad ones—so bad, in fact, that the tenth-century papacy is considered to be the low point of papal history, illustrated best perhaps by Pope John XII (955-63), accused of murder, adultery, incest, castrating a cardinal, and turning the papal palace into a brothel. Whether guilty or not of all of these charges, he was a decidedly dissolute character.

This is the soil in which the roots of the Gregorian reform took hold. Centuries of experience allows us to see this reform movement as a grand effort to delineate distinct boundaries between the secular and temporal realms. We have to bear in mind that early medieval people had never conceived of these spheres as entirely

---

6. Joseph H. Lynch, *The Medieval Church: A Brief History* (London: Longman, 1992), pp. 122-26.

discrete. That is why it seemed natural to them that a king might lead religious reforms and enforce orthodoxy, and a bishop might wield power over vast lands, act as judge in civil disputes, and advise lay lords about secular matters. In the eleventh century, however, just as the Church was beginning to develop as an institution with a network of administrative connections across the western world, and just as fledgling kingdoms and principalities were beginning to develop into what would eventually be known as "states," people began to wonder about the proper spheres of action for popes, bishops, and other ecclesiastics, on the one hand, and emperor, kings, and lay lords, on the other.[7] In other words, for the first time since early Christianity, people began to intuit that there was a clear difference, even a contrast at times, between the things of Caesar and the things of God.

Reform of the clergy and ending lay control over clerical appointments were central to the Gregorian reform. The reform of the clergy included a strong drive to enforce clerical celibacy and stop the practice of simony (the buying and selling of church offices). Behind such reform, we can discern the more subterranean thrust to delineate boundaries between the spiritual and temporal: the things of God (the clergy and clerical offices) were to be preserved from worldly taint (marriage, sex, and commercial transactions). The battle to eliminate laymen from the process of selecting bishops centered on a ceremony in which a lay ruler invested an individual with the office of bishop by giving him the symbols of ring and staff.

Historians often characterize the "investiture conflict," as it became known, as a controversy pitting spiritual churchmen against power-hungry laity. But this view is simplistic. We should note that the Gregorian reform was launched by the pious German king and emperor Henry III (1046-56) who devoted more time to Church

---

7. For the intellectual changes behind this shift, see M.D. Chenu's masterful *Nature, Man, and Society in the Twelfth Century*, trans. Jerome Taylor and Lester K. Little (Toronto: University of Toronto Press, 1997).

reform than he did to politics.[8] It was he who successfully dismissed three rival claimants to the papacy and installed in their stead popes committed to Church reform. His third appointment, Leo IX (1049-54), in an unprecedented move, traveled around Europe holding councils with bishops, abbots, and other dignitaries, pressing them to pass decrees condemning simony, and enforcing clerical celibacy, a discipline still widely ignored. This was the beginning of the Gregorian reform, and an early step in the long process of transforming the bishop of Rome from the symbolic head into the juridical head of all western European bishops. Bearing in mind that Henry III instigated the reform, it is ironic that a subsequent pope, Gregory VII (1073-85), made it a centerpiece of his reform to win the "freedom of the Church" from any kind of lay interference in the selection and appointment of church officials. He also made the new claim that a pope could depose emperors and asserted that his orders were to be received as if they were God's.[9]

Gregory, and popes after him, transformed the Church and the papacy. The once overlapping spheres of sacred and secular rule were indeed becoming separated. Clerical marriage, though still common, declined, as did simony. Priests who heretofore might have been simple peasants tilling the land alongside their neighbors, were gradually developing into a class clearly set apart from—and above—the rest of the population. It is especially worth noting that in their efforts to end lay investiture and do away with the powerful influence of lay lords, kings, and emperors in episcopal appointments, the Gregorian reformers entirely diminished the role of any laity in the selection of bishops. This role had been repeatedly affirmed in church documents and by popes since New Testament times.[10] The

---

8. He was king 1039-1056, emperor 1046-56.

9. For Gregory's views, see the *Dictatus Papae*, in *The Crisis of Church and State, 1050-1300*, ed. Brian Tierney (Englewood, NJ: Prentice-Hall, 1964), pp. 49-50; and *The Correspondence of Pope Gregory VII*, trans. Ephraim Emerton (New York: Columbia University Press, 1990).

10. For a brief and fairly reliable overview, see John E. Lynch, "Appointment of Bishops, History," in *The Papacy: An Encyclopedia* (New York: Routledge, 2002), vol. 1, pp. 90-95.

tradition was explicitly acknowledged by the canonist Gratian in his influential twelfth-century collection of canon law. However, he re-interpreted other early evidence to argue newly that "Lay persons must in no way involve themselves in an election." Gratian justified the new electoral system, which categorically reduced the role of the laity to "*humble* consent" and "obedience," by stating that times had changed.[11] Subsequent popes introduced other changes that dimin-ished the role of the local clergy, and the metropolitan bishop as well. By the pontificate of Urban V (1362-70), the pope reserved the right to fill all episcopal vacancies, thus ending the role of the local clergy and bishops in the election process.[12] These popes built the papacy into the first and most powerful monarchical machine in all of Europe.

Simplistic accounts of the Gregorian reform adopt the papacy's own polemical language: spiritual ecclesiastics fighting to save the Church from power-hungry laity. Neither of these characterizations is true, although there were examples of both pious churchmen and self-interested laymen. But emperors and kings from Charlemagne to Henry III show that Christian laity were at times the very cata-lysts for church reform, promoting good men to church offices, while popes and other prelates sometimes proved the greatest obstacles to achieving a holy Church.

Relevance of the Gregorian Reform and the Investiture Controversy for the Contemporary Church

The first reform I suggest for the contemporary Church is a return to the involvement of the local clergy and laity in the selection of bishops. Certainly the papacy should play an important role in this process, but there seems little justification for excluding the

---

11. *Decretum*, or *Concordance of Discordant Canons*, Distinctions 61-63; Robert L. Benson, *The Bishop-Elect: A Study in Medieval Ecclesiastical Office* (Princeton, NJ: Princeton University Press, 1968), pp. 23-35; emphasis added.

12. Bernhard Schimmelpfennig, *The Papacy*, trans. James Sievert (New York: Columbia University Press, 1992), pp. 204-205.

perspectives of the people and clergy of a diocese. They are best positioned to know their own needs, so we must search for models that restore to them significant authority in the selection process.

Further, I want to underline the critical importance of returning the laity to this process. While it would be naive to assume that lay involvement in the selection of bishops and popes would be a panacea for the ills besetting church leadership today, the past proves that lay participation is deeply part of our tradition in very positive ways. The involvement of laymen and women in the selection of worthy men—and soon, one hopes, women—to leadership positions will be not only a catalyst for Church reform, but also an instance of the very reform we need. Just as Gratian argued that changed times call for changes in the mode of selecting bishops, so too should we acknowledge that an increasingly democratic world and collegial Church require the participation of lay people in the selection of their Church leaders.

This is particularly so in light of the fact that, in many parts of the world, lay people today enjoy a level of education and theological awareness unprecedented in history. Indeed, whereas all medieval theologians were ecclesiastics and the majority of lay people were illiterate, in the contemporary American Church the majority of Catholic theologians are lay people. Increasingly, our parish ministries also are occupied by laymen and women with Catholic ministerial degrees equivalent to those earned by the ordained clergy. The Catholic laity in the United States are now prominent in all the professions and rank among the most highly educated people in the country. Their participation in the selection of bishops would harken back to and well beyond the medieval Church, for lay participation today would involve not only the most powerful members of lay society but, in the words of Clement to the Corinthians, the voice and "consent of the whole Church."[13]

History shows that the selection of good bishops depended neither on the lay nor clerical status of those making the choice. Rather,

---

13. *First Epistle of Clement to the Corinthians* 44; written about AD 96.

good selections were—and will in the future—be made by good people, devoted to the Church and committed to the Christian life, regardless of their status.

The Evangelical Awakening of the Laity

While the Gregorian reform movement involved primarily the elites of society, such as lay rulers and church prelates, there was another sort of reform movement underway about the same time that concerned people from humbler social strata. Until about the year 1000, we know relatively little about these men and women despite the fact that they constituted the vast majority of Christians. It goes without saying that they had no influence in the selection of bishops, abbesses, abbots, and other ecclesiastics during the medieval period. They did, however, participate in the devotional life of the Church. Their children would be baptized, for example, and they celebrated ecclesial feast days with fellow villagers and peasants. Busy as they were with the business of survival, bereft of a decent education, ministered to by priests with only a rudimentary knowledge of the faith, most lay people were fortunate to know a few prayers in Latin and be able to explain the Creed. Their faith life might be deep, but their influence in Church matters was virtually nil.

All this began to change in the eleventh century. A host of favorable changes improved living standards. Better weather, for example, led to more productive agriculture. More food led to longer lives and boosted population growth. Better security against outside invaders like the Vikings boosted trade and population. Towns and cities abandoned since the fall of the Roman empire reemerged and others were founded. Commerce stepped up and a new middle class of merchants, peddlers, and craftspeople appeared.

Hand in hand with this social and economic renaissance was a veritable efflorescence of religious piety that inspired an array of pious lay movements. People were fired with zeal for what they referred to as the "*vita apostolica*"—the apostolic life. Imitating the life of the apostles, for them, meant a life of poverty, sharing goods in common, preaching the good news, helping the needy, and doing works of penance. Although historians cannot be sure of all the reasons behind this flowering of lay piety, it is clear that town life provided more schools, greater access to the Scriptures and to quality preaching. At the same time, city life also highlighted the new extremes of wealth and poverty, motivating many newly prosperous Christians to renounce their wealth and help their needy neighbors.

This was a sea change in Christian life. Prior to the year 1000, one might speak of a few very wealthy elite and then masses of much humbler and sometimes desperately poor people. The very few rich governed, and everyone else obeyed. Spiritually, there was a parallel divide. The spiritual elites were the monks, nuns, and higher clergy. Serious dedication to a holy Christian life was considered beyond the reach of the great mass of simple laity, tainted as they were by "worldly" cares. Now, for the first time in centuries, we begin to see members of the emerging middle class assume roles of authority in city governance. It was not a democracy, but it was more participative. Spiritually, we note a parallel movement as thousands of ordinary women and men dedicated themselves to the pursuit of Christian perfection. They included mothers and fathers, shopkeepers and housekeepers, cobblers and seamstresses. Some pursued the holy life as individuals, while others joined loosely defined movements or specific religious groups. Religious life was no longer the preserve of monks and nuns. Now piety could be for everybody. It was a revolution.

And it took many forms. It included parish or craft-based confraternities or sodalities that combined devotion to a patron saint with some good works and social festivities. Other groups were more amorphous and constituted broad "movements" rather than specific organizations, just as today we might speak of a "peace movement," a catch-all term describing an array of individuals and groups. The Brothers and Sisters of Penance was a widespread movement of lay people who variously committed themselves to a life of prayer, good works, and personal penitential practices. A remarkable number of lay people gave all their worldly goods to the poor. Some married people renounced all sexual activity, believing it interfered with their love of God.[14]

How did the institutional church react to all this? In many different ways—it was, after all, an unprecedented phenomenon and, as such, ecclesiastics were variously negotiating their responses to the situation. There were churchmen who celebrated and encouraged these groups, while others reacted with disdain or even fear. Assessing these reactions is not a simple matter of "good guys" and "bad guys." Such a massive "evangelical awakening," as the great Catholic theologian and historian M.D. Chenu describes it, gave churchmen great pause.

Textbook accounts of this period place Francis of Assisi (c. 1182-1226) center stage, sometimes portraying him as the founder of this vast movement of lay piety. After all, Francis was himself a layman and he attracted to himself thousands of lay followers hoping to imitate the apostolic life. But Francis is the culmination of this movement, rather than its originator. Individuals like Francis, and male and female groups similar to the Franciscan friars, had been struggling, with little success, for a place within the Church for well over a century when Pope Innocent III (1198-1216) finally had the visionary audacity to extend formal recognition to Francis and his followers. Francis's radical vision of material poverty and humility was, in part, less threatening to the pope because Francis enthusiastically endorsed the papacy and, although reluctant, he also agreed to institutionalize his movement of laymen into the Franciscan order.

There were, however, dozens of groups besides the Franciscans, both before and after Francis, who were not so fortunate. We tend to forget about these groups because they did not survive. History is written, so the saying goes, by the winners, and their narratives overshadow the accounts of less successful groups. The stories of these

---

14. For a discussion of some of these groups, see Lester K. Little, *Religious Poverty and the Profit Economy in Medieval Europe* (Ithaca, NY: Cornell University Press, 1978), pp. 113-34; and Chenu, *Nature, Man and Society*, pp. 219-69.

forgotten men and women, however, can draw our attention to over-looked and underestimated constituencies in the Church today.

Several novel features of this evangelical awakening that made it a breath of fresh air to many of the faithful, and an ill wind to some members of the hierarchy, are worth noting. First, it was a religious life "in the world." Although priests and other religious were also involved in this awakening, many groups were predominantly lay. Second, some of these lay people preached on street corners and in town plazas, freely offering their own interpretations of Scripture and church life. Bishops and other clerics worried that uneducated lay people were ill-prepared to preach. Indeed, a host of heretical teachings sprang up that had to be countered. Popes and bishops vacillated on whether or not to grant the license to preach to these groups. Some refused in principle ever to allow lay preaching, no matter how orthodox. One feature of lay preaching that particularly rankled many prelates were lay critiques of clerical wealth and privilege. The men and women who adopted the *vita apostolica* believed that imitating the apostles required personal poverty and generous sharing of all material goods. They denounced the high lifestyle, palatial residences, and haughty demeanor of many churchmen. Prelates were shocked at these frontal assaults and some used their power to quash such groups.

A third feature merits a fuller discussion: the prominence of women as participants in these movements. Like their male counterparts, laywomen reflected on the gospel and offered their own interpretations of the Christian life; they undertook charitable works in the streets of cities rather than remaining at home; and some even preached. A notable movement of such women evident in north-central Europe by the late twelfth century was the Beguines. Beguines supported themselves by the work of their hands. They lived in their own homes, alone or in small groups. They led poor and celibate lives, but made no formal vows and could quit at any time. They had no founder, no superior, no male clerical supervisor, or church oversight of any type. No overarching institutional structure united the many small groups that dotted the towns and cities. Beguines were the first, large-scale women's movement in European history, sur-passing ten percent of the adult female population in some cities.[15]

At first, they were warmly, even enthusiastically received by some clerics. Popes Honorius III in 1216 and Gregory IX in 1233 warmly approved Beguine life.[16] The Cistercian Caesarius of Heisterbach (c. 1180-1240) claimed Beguines loved God more than many who lived in the cloister and would receive a greater crown in heaven.[17] As their numbers grew, however, even though the majority were quite orthodox and never preached, popes, bishops, and town councillors became increasingly alarmed. Women on their own, without any male supervision, were simply intolerable in medieval society.[18] In-exorably, Beguines who pursued the devout life individually or in small numbers, without a rule or ecclesiastical supervision, were variously outlawed, condemned as heretics, or forced into other lifestyles. The Beguines who survived were those willing to live ac-cording to a rule, in organized groups and institutions known as beguinages, under a superior and submissive to church authorities in all matters. Other regulations heaped upon them restricted their movements in and out of the beguinages, limited their contact with men, prescribed what they should wear, including a veil, curtailed their activities, and encouraged them toward an essentially contem-plative lifestyle. In short, the "beguines" who survived had become very much like nuns.[19]

---

15. Walter Simons, *Cities of Ladies: Beguine Communities in the Medieval Low Countries, 1200-1565* (Philadelphia: University of Pennsylvania Press, 2001), p. 60; Caroline Walker Bynum, *Holy Feast and Holy Fast: The Religious Significance of Food to Medieval Women* (Berkeley, CA: University of California Press, 1987), p. 18. Simons' study is the best work to date on the beguines.

16. For Honorius, see Jacques de Vitry's Letter 74, in *Lettres de Jacques de Vitry (1160/ 1170-1240), évêque de Saint-Jean d'Acre*, ed. R.B.C. Huygens (Leiden: E.J. Brill, 1960); for Gregory, see his bull, *Gloriam virginalem*.

17. Simons, *Cities of Ladies*, p. 35.

18. Anke Passenier, "'Women on the Loose': Stereotypes of Women in the Story of the Medieval Beguines," in *Female Stereotypes in Religious Traditions*, eds. Ria Kloppenborg and Wouter J. Hannegraaff (Leiden: E.J. Brill, 1995).

19. Simons, *Cities of Ladies*, pp. 118-37.

Other women's groups generally followed this same pattern, eventually being forced to take vows and join one of the approved religious orders. In 1298, Pope Boniface VIII decreed strict claustration for all nuns.[20] Male groups fared better. Even though men, like women, were gradually pressured to accept full ecclesiastical supervision, they were allowed to remain "in the world" to pray, preach, and perform good works, thus creating a vital new religious alternative to male monastic life.

Relevance of the Lay Evangelical Awakening for the Contemporary Church

This revolutionary stage in Church history of a lay evangelical awakening—a period that gave us confraternities, sodalities, lay calls for reform of the church hierarchy, and what we now recognize as "apostolic" religious orders dedicated to a life of prayer and work "in the world"—teaches us that the Spirit often moves and speaks most discernibly in the community of faithful at large. I suggest that all of us, and especially the hierarchy, need to listen more carefully today to what the Spirit is saying to the Church through the laity. This requires a structured place for the voice of the laity within the government of the Church, with accountability on all sides.

More broadly, one might extend this point about the laity having an effective voice within the Church to other levels of church governance. Vatican II spawned a host of advisory bodies with no real authority at various levels throughout the Church, ranging from parish councils advising their pastors, diocesan pastoral councils advising bishops, to national and international bodies of bishops advising the pope. The past decades of experimentation with this form of voluntary collegiality have shown it to be ineffectual. In each case, it is left to the person being advised, be he the pope, bishop, or pastor, to do what he will with the advice proffered. Important

---

20. Boniface VIII, *Periculoso*, in Elizabeth Makowski, *Canon Law and Cloistered Women: Periculoso and Its Commentators, 1298-1545* (Washington, D.C.: Catholic University of America Press, 1997), pp. 133-36.

insights—some practical with regard to administration and management, some substantive regarding church discipline, some theological regarding our faith—are too often ignored by those who exercise actual juridic authority. Specifically with regard to the laity, if their insights are truly valued, then the structure of decision-making in the Church should reflect that by giving them genuine authority with accountability.

I further suggest that women's voices be accorded as much respect and be given as much weight as men's voices at every level of church life—in our parishes, in dioceses, in assemblies and conferences, and in church councils. Having kept the faith through centuries of subordination and forced supervision, women—and the many men who recognize women as full partners in faith and ministry—should neither remain silent themselves nor be silenced by others. The Beguines are simply one example of dozens in the history of our Church that illustrate the ways in which women's ministry and gifts have been unjustifiably suppressed. In virtually every sphere of life today, from family to business to politics, women's equality has been recognized and men and women alike have benefited. How long must we wait for the hierarchical church to stop leaning on theological formulations rejected by the vast majority of Catholic theologians and Scripture scholars to justify their monopoly on the ministry and their exclusion of women from the table of decision-making? We need to acknowledge forthrightly that this is an issue that is simply not going to go away. Orders that come down from on high forbidding laity and clergy alike even to discuss issues such as women's ordination are both counterproductive and infantalizing. The first step in the right direction will be for the hierarchy to lift its ill-conceived and embarrassing attempt at censorship and engage in an open discussion of these issues with the laity and parish clergy.

The Conciliar Movement

Another illuminating example of Church reform is the "conciliar movement," which flourished roughly from about 1300 to 1550. Although conciliar theory had many variants, in the main it advocated the establishment of a mixed constitutional form of government within the Church, with participation by all, and special authority vested in general church councils.

This movement stands in stark contrast with the trend toward papal monarchy set in motion by Pope Gregory VII and developed by subsequent popes such as Innocent III (1198-1216) and Boniface VIII (1294-1303). In a papal bull some scholars see as the quintessential expression of papal supremacy, Boniface asserted that the pope's power included even the temporal authority of secular rulers, and that no one could be saved who was not subject to him.[21] Ironically, the very claims made to buttress papal power also worked to undermine it. Cardinals and bishops alike, for example, thought the increasingly centralized power of the papacy diminished their own proper roles. Drawing on Scripture, tradition, and canon law, theorists began to argue for a more corporate view of church authority that included the cardinals and bishops.[22]

Although there were some excellent popes in this period, several events in particular contributed to a serious decline in papal prestige and authority. The popes' ongoing battles with secular kings such as Philip the Fair of France over jurisdictional issues put papal supremacy front and center as a topic of debate among canon lawyers, theologians, and others, and this in turn led some thinkers to develop critiques of papal claims to power.

Two other events were particularly devastating. First, Philip the Fair managed to secure the election of his own candidate, the archbishop of Bordeaux, to the papacy. The new French pope, Clement V (1305-14), then capitulated to Philip's request that he abandon Rome, the symbolic heart of the Church, to reside instead at Avignon, a papal estate just across the river from France. During an almost seventy-year period known as the "Babylonian Captivity" (1309-77),

---

21. *Unam sanctam* (1302).

22. Brian Tierney, *Foundations of the Conciliar Theory: The Contribution of the Medieval Canonists From Gratian to the Great Schism*, 2d ed. (Leiden: E.J. Brill, 1998), esp. pt. 3, chap. 2.

the popes—all French—remained in Avignon.[23] The Church quickly became more French than universal: of 134 new cardinals appointed by the popes, 113 were French.

The popes of Avignon established a mighty legal and financial bureaucracy that concentrated the Church's vast power and wealth within the papal court, or "curia." Most revenues came from the sale of indulgences and, especially, taxes charged for benefices. A benefice was typically a right granted to a cleric appointed to a church position entitling him to receive income from church property attached to the position. Historically, the right to grant ecclesiastical positions with benefices had belonged to members of the laity and ecclesiastics such as bishops and abbots. However, the popes had won full control of these appointments by the time they were residing at Avignon. These popes and the papal curia granted literally thousands of benefices each year, often to petitioners unknown to the papacy, and often to individuals known to be unworthy, including papal nephews and grasping nobles.[24] To most people, this looked just like simony: the pope was selling church offices. The papacy had become a profitable patronage machine. Although some of the popes at Avignon are known to have led personally austere lives, many members of the curia, including many cardinals, led self-indulgent lives in scandalously opulent surroundings. Devout Christians implored the popes to sever their French ties. Catherine of Siena (1347-80) even traveled to Avignon and was instrumental in persuading Gregory XI (1370-78) finally to return to Rome in 1377.[25]

Gregory died the next year, which launched a second disastrous interlude for the papacy. Italian citizens, fearful that another French pope would again abandon Rome, successfully urged the largely

---

23. Petrarch (1304-74) coined the phrase "Babylonian Captivity."

24. Geoffrey Barraclough, *Papal Provisions* (Oxford: Blackwell, 1935), pp. 104-105; Walter Ullmann, *A Short History of the Papacy in the Middle Ages* (London: Routledge, 2003), p. 287.

25. Among her forceful letters to him, see Letters 54, 69, 74, 76, 77, 81, 88 in *The Letters of St. Catherine of Siena*, trans. Suzanne Noffke, vol. 1 (Binghamton, NY: Center Medieval and Early Renaissance Studies, 1988).

French college of cardinals to elect an Italian as pope. The new Pope Urban VI (1378-98) began a highly undiplomatic reform of the curia and immediately alienated his electors with blistering denunciations and threats. The cardinals fled the city, proclaimed the election invalid, and elected a Frenchman as Pope Clement VII (1378-94). Thus began the Great Western Schism, with two men claiming to be pope and all of Europe bitterly divided in their allegiances. A Parisian theologian hit the mark when he said, "Not even a hardened heart can be unmoved at the sight of holy mother church in such agony."[26] For ordinary Christians, who also suffered many famines, wars, and plagues in the fourteenth century, the institution they counted on to console them had become a source of distress and scandal. Papal prestige plummeted; some people's faith wavered; and many Christians became openly critical of the church as an institution.

These two events led many medieval thinkers to question the assumption that monarchy was the most perfect form of church government. Already in the thirteenth century, Thomas Aquinas, although not explicitly discussing the Church, had argued that the best form of government was a mixed constitution that combined features of democracy and aristocracy with monarchical rule.[27] Other theorists, commenting specifically on papal misuse of temporal power, went further. Marsiglio of Padua (1275-1342), writing anonymously during the Avignon papacy, used Scripture and the Church Fathers to argue that the pope was not divinely empowered to guide kings and reign supreme over all society. Just as Christ had refused rulership for himself (and his apostles) to devote himself to spiritual affairs, so too should the popes and other prelates. Marsiglio, in fact, thought the Church should relinquish all its temporal power

---

26. Cited in F. Donald Logan, *A History of the Church in the Middle Ages* (London: Routledge, 2002), p. 316.

27. Brian Tierney, "Church Law and Alternative Structures: A Medieval Perspective," paper delivered at the conference "Governance, Accountability and the Future of the Catholic Church," St. Thomas More Chapel, Yale University, March 28, 2003.

and submit to the rule of the state, just as Christ had submitted himself to the judgement of Pilate.[28] A few years after publishing these ideas, Marsiglio was declared a heretic.

The respected twelfth-century bishop and canonist Huguccio set the course for the more moderate mainstream conciliarists. He distinguished between the universal Church, that is, the whole collection of the faithful, founded and protected by Christ, and the Roman Church, comprised of pope and cardinals, who could be sinners and even heretics as history showed. Although authority of a certain type was entrusted to Peter and his successors, Christ's full authority was given only to the whole Church. Divine protection from all error was a gift made not to the hierarchical church, but to the community of the faithful in its entirety. By the fourteenth century, even advocates of papal authority defined the Church as a juridical corporate entity of all the faithful. It was only logical then for theologians, bishops, cardinals, and canonists to place a church council above the pope, and to advocate a mixed constitution as the best form of church government.[29] It is important to bear in mind that far from attacking the papacy, these theologians, some who would themselves later become popes, were trying to restore the papacy, unify the Church, and protect it. They drew on Scripture, the Church Fathers, and canon law to make their arguments.

Despite plentiful efforts to resolve the schism, neither pope would step down and recognize the other, and neither would convene a council to settle the matter. It would take a church council, more and more churchmen argued, to resolve the matter of a divided papacy and Christendom. Finally, some twenty years into the schism, the cardinals from both sides took matters into their own hands. They deserted their respective popes and convened the Council of Pisa in 1409. There, acting as an authority above the papacy, they deposed both claimants and elected Alexander V. When the

---

28. *The Defender of the Peace*, trans. Alan Gewirth (New York: Columbia University Press, 1956).

29. Tierney, *Foundations of Conciliar Theory*, pp. 37-42, 182-86, 199-214.

first two men refused to be deposed, however, the schism continued, now with three competing popes. It finally ended in 1417, almost four decades after it had begun, when the Council of Constance convened and successfully removed all three papal claimants, then elected Martin V.

The council issued two particularly memorable decrees. The first, *Haec sancta* (1415—also known as *Sacrosancta*), made conciliarism the official teaching of the Church by declaring that the council received its authority directly from Christ and that its power was superior to that of a pope alone. The second, *Frequens* (1417), decreed that councils be held every ten years to ensure the welfare of the Church, and it importantly included a mechanism for convening a council if the pope refused to summon it.[30] Although historians consider these decrees revolutionary, the council members saw their actions as conservative: they were simply turning the Church away from the monarchical and absolutist trends begun in the Gregorian reform and returning it to the balanced and conciliar form of government prevalent in the Church during its first one thousand years.[31] In these centuries, councils defined dogmas, denounced heresies, and healed schisms.

The Council of Constance saved the papacy, but the popes were loath to accept its reforms. The status of the two decrees is still debated. On the one hand, the Council of Constance had been convoked by Pope John XXIII, a successor of the third pope elected at the Council of Pisa and recognized at the time as the legitimate pope, so the council's decrees were valid.[32] On the other hand, although

---

30. The first council was to meet five years after the end of the Council of Constance; the next council seven years after that; and subsequent councils were to meet every ten years.

31. Norman P. Tanner, *The Councils of the Church: A Short History* (New York: Crossroad, 2001), pp. 68-69.

32. John XXIII would later be deposed, a circumstance no one invoked to question the validity of the Council of Constance's decrees. Further, Benedict XIII, whom the Catholic Church now judges to have been the "true" pope, convoked the council for a second time after John's deposition (after *Haec sancta*, but before *Frequens* had been issued).

the new pope elected by the Council of Constance, Martin V, never openly challenged the decrees (especially since his own election depended on the council's validity), he and subsequent popes resisted them. Over the next century they managed to reverse the tide of the conciliar movement. In 1460, in fact, Pope Pius II (formerly a conciliarist himself) condemned conciliar theory and reaffirmed papal supremacy.[33] Nevertheless, significant and mainstream theologians in subsequent centuries continued to accept arguments in favor of conciliar and mixed constitutional modes of governance. It is only since Vatican I (1869-70), noted for its definitions of papal primacy and infallibility, that conciliar theory has been misleadingly portrayed as a passing historical anomaly.[34]

Relevance of the Conciliar Movement for the Contemporary Church

The central questions raised during the conciliar movement have never been adequately resolved. Vatican II's affirmation of the essentially collegial nature of the Church pointed to new models of collaboration and communion which we are still searching to define. I suggest that the present crisis of leadership within the Church, which has so strained the communion and trust between the laity and hierarchy, makes this a most propitious moment for a full discussion of these questions. Where does Christ's authority reside in the Church? What should the right relationship be among Peter, the apostles, and the people of God? How does the Holy Spirit speak through the universal Church? How do the various constituencies in the Church listen to the Spirit speaking through other members? How are the voices of these constituencies adequately represented? How are disagreements between a particular constituency, such as a

---

33. In his bull *Execrabilis* (18 January 1460).

34. Francis Oakley, "Constitutionalism in the Church?" paper delivered at the conference "Governance, Accountability and the Future of the Catholic Church," St. Thomas More Chapel, Yale University, March 28, 2003. On conciliar tradition through Vatican I, see Oakley's *The Conciliarist Tradition: Constitutionalism in the Catholic Church, 1300-1870* (New York: Oxford University Press, 2003).

national council of bishops, and the Roman curia resolved? How can we promote the participation of all constituencies within the Church while yet preserving our unity?

A very popular refrain today of some opponents of Church reform is that the "Church is not a democracy." I wonder, do they mean to imply that the Church is meant to be a monarchy? or an aristocracy? These positions are at least as untenable as an argument for democracy alone. The conciliarists certainly were not arguing for a democratic form of government in the Church and neither are the vast majority of Catholics desirous of a more participative mode of church governance today. A mixed form of government, however, including the pope, bishops, and the laity, is not only in order, but well supported by the Church's earliest traditions and a long line of theological reflection.

The Council of Trent's Reform of the Episcopacy

My fourth and final topic, drawn from a church council marking the end of the medieval period and the beginning of the modern world, is necessarily brief given the scope of this essay. However, I can hardly pass over in silence the momentous Council of Trent, called in the sixteenth century, in the wake of the Protestant Reformation, with the dual aim of reforming the Church and reaffirming Catholic doctrine. In keeping with the purpose of this essay, I will focus on the council's reforming efforts.

The term "reform" itself, adopted by Trent, suggests discontinuity with the past; something has gone wrong and needs to be set right. It was, in fact, the Gregorian reform, which predated the Council of Trent by five hundred years, that first introduced the notion that the entire Church—not just this or that heretical individual or wayward cleric—might be in need of reform. Between the eleventh century and Trent, there were repeated complaints about the moral conduct of priests, about bishops being absent from their dioceses or simultaneously heading multiple dioceses simply for the sake of gaining more revenues. At the time of the Western Schism, the Council of Constance explicitly declared that there should be a reform of the entire Church, "in faith and morals," and "in head and members."[35] Widespread recognition of the need for the reform of priests, bishops, and the papacy had, in fact, fueled the Protestant Reformation.

It is worth noting that the Council of Trent first convened in 1545, a full twenty-eight years after Luther posted his Ninety-five Theses. Catholic historian Hubert Jedin is among those who contend that this was simply too late for Lutheranism to be checked as a minor heresy.[36] One significant reason for the delay was the fear popes had of sharing their authority with a council: memories of the conciliar movement were still fresh.

The reform proposed by the council, although more circumscribed than a reform of the entire Church, had far-reaching consequences. It aimed to reform the morals "of the clergy and Christian people," essentially, through a reform of three offices in the church: the papacy, the episcopacy, and the pastorate of pastors and parishes. It failed to reform the papacy, primarily because the pope and his legates at the council resisted reform. Its reform of the episcopacy, however, was extensive, and comprehended even the reform of the pastorate because the supervision of pastors and their parishes was made the clear responsibility of bishops.[37]

Stereotypic dismissals of the Council of Trent as a merely reactionary council miss the tremendously positive results of its thorough treatment of the proper role of the bishop. The reform is remarkable in part because it was an instance of bishops reforming themselves. They not only condemned episcopal abuses such as failing to reside in their dioceses and holding multiple bishoprics, but

---

35. John W. O'Malley, "Reform, Historical Consciousness, and Vatican II's *Aggiornamento*," in *Tradition and Transition: Historical Perspectives on Vatican II* (Wilmington, DE: Michael Glazier, 1989), pp. 52-55.

36. *A History of the Council of Trent*, trans. Ernst Graf, vol. 1 (St. Louis: Herder, 1957), p. 580.

37. John W. O'Malley, "The Council of Trent: Myths, Misunderstandings, and Misinformation," in *Spirit, Style, Story: Essays Honoring John W. Padberg, S.J.*, ed. Thomas M. Lucas (Chicago: Jesuit Way/Loyola, 2002), pp. 209-210, 214.

also elaborated and insisted upon the bishop's essentially sacramental and pastoral role. This was reform indeed. The bishop was, for example, to preach to his people and to give an example through his own life. He was to carefully screen candidates for the priesthood, provide them with solid training, then assiduously supervise their pastoral work and personal conduct. He was to meet annually in synod with his priests and visit regularly the institutions throughout his diocese. The bishop was transformed from a collector of benefices to a pastor of souls.[38] Change was slow, but Trent's attention to the role of the bishop gradually yielded positive fruit in a reformed episcopacy.

Relevance of the Council of Trent's Episcopal Reform for the Contemporary Church

The situation of bishops today is very different from that of bishops at the time of the Council of Trent. Vatican II's decree on bishops, *Christus Dominus*, had no need to address a long list of episcopal abuses as did the Council of Trent. A stark similarity, however, is that today, just as then, there is a distinct need to revisit the role of the bishop. It is by no means an affront to the office of bishop, or to the good work of so many individual bishops around the world today, to call for a reform of the episcopate, or at least certain features of it. Church councils besides Trent, not to mention many other local reforms throughout history, have had reason to reassess the office of bishop.

Today is clearly another such moment, the failures of so many bishops having been painfully brought into the light of day: the failure over decades to protect the innocent lives of hundreds, probably thousands, of children; the failure to supervise, discipline, and obtain proper help for abusive priests; the failure to be open and honest about what has transpired; the failure to courageously reject the

---

38. O'Malley, "The Council of Trent," in *Spirit, Style, Story*, pp. 214-17; the characterization of bishops as collectors of benefices and pastors of souls belongs to Hubert Jedin, cited in O'Malley, p. 214

culture of clericalism that valued reputation and secrecy more highly than people's lives. We must ask: To whom is a bishop accountable for the fulfillment of his duties? Does he answer only to the pope? or should he answer also to the people and clergy? In what ways is he accountable to the people of the diocese for the conduct of priests? or for the administration of the diocese, including the management of the laity's money? Do the trappings of episcopal office work to insulate a bishop from the life of the people? Do the burdens of financial and administrative cares diminish his attention to teaching and preaching? What responsibilities do the people bear regarding the bishop, his well-being, and the good running of the diocese? What is the bishop's relationship with and responsibility to the priests of the diocese? Is he chief executive, spiritual guide, father, brother, or some combination of these? Together, in an open forum involving lay people, priests, and bishops, we need to discuss these and other questions to strengthen the bishops as leaders and pastors.

I further suggest that this would be a useful time for a full and open discussion of the role of the papacy. Although it was initially envisioned that the role of the pope, and the ills besetting the papacy, would be fully discussed and constitute another of the reforms of the Council of Trent, this never came to pass. In light of papal history both prior to the Reformation and afterwards, this omission is unfortunate. The monarchical papacy that we have today began to take shape with the Gregorian reform early in the second millennium years of our history. Debates about it have continued on and off in all the centuries since then.

Specifically with regard to bishops, the promise of collegiality between pope and bishops suggested by Vatican II perdures more in hope than in reality. Today, the papacy and curial officials dominate many important decisions that should involve more advice and guidance from bishops around the world who, after all, have concrete experience of the realities confronting their dioceses. Vatican II appeared intent on strengthening and expanding the pastoral authority of bishops. However, bishops today, in many respects, seem increasingly to be mere rubber stamps for the papacy and curia, mouthpieces for decisions and policies made in a top-down fashion.

Conclusion

These four moments of Church reform establish clearly that there have been many modes of church governance and organization through the centuries. It is an institutional myth, an unconvincing justification of the status quo, to maintain that what is today always was and was always meant to be. At every level of the Church today, from pope, to bishops, to priests, to people, we are being called to search for more participative, collegial models of being Church. Far from being a novelty, this search will return us in important ways to the earliest models of church governance. History, however, never simply repeats itself; history is about change. Each age poses a new configuration of promises and challenges. The task before us, then, is to read the signs of *these* times, confident that God is present in our history, guiding us in our moment to be the Church God desires. Great conflict is often the catalyst for great creativity. With the Spirit's help, may it be so in our Church today.

4. What Can We Learn From the Tridentine and Baroque Church?

Rev. Thomas F. O'Meara, O.P., University of Notre Dame

The Baroque is the most recent, completed period in Catholic history, and as such it touches both the past and the present. To consider the time from Trent to Vatican II is to face the challenge of presenting the past and the present, brilliance and decline, renewal and meager restoration.

The term, "the Baroque," stands for the Catholic Church's immediate past, a time of several centuries. The Baroque was preceded by the Council of Trent and followed by Rococo. The Baroque had two lives: the brilliant forms of the sixteenth and seventeenth centuries flourished on an international scale, and then it appeared anew from 1830 to 1960. In the past twenty years, often what one has heard to bear the label "conservative" (actually all Catholics are conservative) or to bear the label "some old Roman Catholic practice" is neither patristic nor medieval but a pious action or image from 1650 or 1850. Baroque Catholicism perdured to Vatican II. Only American Catholics over fifty years of age have experienced the world of the Baroque and the nineteenth century. For instance, curious rituals and sacral objects at a solemn high Mass, devotions and novenas, multiple visions of Mary, exposition of the Eucharist but not the reception of Communion, terse and automatic theological principles limited to Latin textbooks for seminarians.

What was the Baroque?

The Baroque experiences God in God's limitless breadth and freedom, in God's goodness flowing into the world. The world is experienced in an unexpected diversity and breadth (the movement of spherical earth, oceans, discovery of lands unknown to Europeans), but also in order and arrangement. Christ's humanity with a wide redemptive love is communicated through the pictorializations of the Spiritual Exercises

or the image of the Sacred Heart.[1] Mary assumes a number of repre-
sentations with different clothes and symbols, ranging from Lepanto
to Guadalupe. The Mass and sacraments exalt the real presence but
are not quite what we today call liturgy. Devotions to past saints are
prominent because they are in the vernacular and permit some participation in praying and singing. Private spiritual direction is important but is accompanied by decreasing awareness of and involvement in the variety of people and pressing social problems. Preaching
is not frequent in the parish but there are compensating, if occasional, parish missions. In the Baroque age, spirituality was central.
New schools and methods of prayer and meditations support the
individual, in new religious orders in Europe and in new foreign
missions. Large churches are for pilgrimages or private prayer but
are not really suited to a community's life and liturgy.[2]

Prominence is given to learned societies over traditional universities, to lay fraternities or new clerical congregations over monasteries and priories. As those two periods move toward an end, in
the 1700s toward the French Revolution and in the 1900s toward
Vatican II, the ethos of the Church is not so much ministry or creative evangelism but an anthropology of submission and obedience,
as the papacy draws to itself more and more authority and control.[3]
With considerable success in vitalizing the Church of the past, the
Baroque has three characteristics: 1. individual, 2. mechanics, 3. theater.

In the *Spiritual Exercises*, the writings of Pierre de Bérulle, etc.,

---

1. L. Lenhart, "Barock, Kirchengeschichte," *Lexikon für Theologie und Kirche* (1959), pp. 1, 1258-1260; F. Stegmüller, "Barock, Theologie," Ibid., pp. 1262-63.

2. Lenhart, p. 1258.

3. "The dominant ecclesiological values of the pontifical documents [after 1870]. Historical and eschatological observations are lacking as is also any dialectic between the
'already' and the 'not yet.' An explicit anthropology of submission and obedience is
communicated by them. If authority is exercised well, then order will be assured. This
order is unitary and ultimately hierocratic. The pope occupies the summit of the pyra-
mid and thus finds himself the principle of unity, the norm, and the one who speaks for
the whole church." Yves Congar, *L'Église de Saint Augustin à l'époque moderne* (Paris:
Cerf, 1970), p. 425.

we find methods of prayer for nuns and priests. In all of them, the individual is central. (Of course, the founder of modern philosophy, Descartes, and the later French and American Revolutions strengthen this.) The individual has a life, a calling, a dialogue with God, a vivid story. Converting grace becomes a power within my life, a force assisting me as an individual to avoid my temptations and to follow God's will for me. In countless churches, people are pictured—people ranging from the persons of the Trinity, angels, and biblical figures, to founders and mystics and martyrs. They proclaim the union of the visible and invisible.

Galileo and Newton and the mathematicization of natural science show a cultural shift. Central to Baroque Christianity is a mechanics of actual graces. Actual grace is a transient force, indiscriminate, intrinsically the same; it is an extrinsic power suspended between the divine and the human. The Church becomes a kind of religious electric company, distributing divine forces to adolescent decisions, to reception of important sacraments like marriage and orders, to death-bed decisions. What is of interest in the sacraments is their automatic bringing of grace surrounded by casuistic confessional practice, personal spiritual direction, and church law and administration.

The Baroque world is a theater: buildings, city squares, and baldachinos, spaces set off for human performances whether solemn conclusions of pilgrimages, a palatial reception, or an opera. Emotion is prominent, and art aims at portraying dramatic human gestures and scenes. The Christian life becomes manifest in extraordinary events like conversions, visions, stigmata, ecstasies, asceticism. The Baroque has its own "liturgies," not so much the Eucharist and the seven sacraments, but processions, benediction of the Blessed Sacrament, blessing with relics, rites invoking patronal saints to bless boats or horses. Ultimately, the Church's liturgies serve silent and private meditation with its own emotions and experiences.

Who, we might ask, was "the Church"? The enclosed mystic, the distant missionary, the pope, saints who are past men and women present in visions or art.

The Baroque lived on a second time in the nineteenth century and in the twentieth century up until Vatican II. Why? After the cold distance of the Enlightenment and the violence of the French Revolution of the eighteenth century, Baroque Catholicism found the next cultural period, Romanticism, to be congenial—a mystical and personal approach to life and religion similar to the Baroque. Church life from 1830 to 1950 saw the foundation of one hundred new religious congregations, the emergence of the entire enterprise of active religious women, a papacy which was drawing all power to itself. There were new devotions to the saints (each religious order, each country had its own). In art or piety, a Baroque style perdured. The time from 1830 to Vatican II is the only period of the immediate past which Catholics have known; it is the period before the Council.

Beyond the Baroque

The Baroque period was transcended by Vatican II, by theology, liturgy, and church life prepared for by decades of theological and pastoral renewal in Europe.

Baroque individualism was balanced by the quest for community in parish and diocese and religious order; the liturgy was no longer passive souls watching priestly acts or reading devotions while a rapid, silent Mass was read somewhere in the church, but the public, active, and communal participation of people and ministers in God's presence through sacrament and word. Grace was no longer seen as an occasional force but a perduring life: according to patristic and medieval theologies, grace was a share in Trinitarian life, a life brought by baptism, a life capable of acting within the complexities of secular society, a life that normally ended in some ministry on behalf of the Kingdom of God. Liturgy and ministry aimed primarily not at the fulfillment of canon law but at the expansion of a parish. Social problems, personal difficulties, new issues in family and medicine, degrees of grace in people living in large Western cities, and salvation in the variety of religions in the East—all this made a Christianity that was mainly an "electric company" or a "theater" irrelevant. In 1968, Henri Denis described how Vatican II altered and restored the basic reality of the priesthood.[4] That ministry expanded from the solitary priest's silent celebration of the Eucharist (joined to the congregation at the time of elevation) to a complexity of ministries in parish and diocese. The specificity of the presbyter lies no longer solely in the power to consecrate bread and wine but to act in various ways in the power of the risen Christ, precisely for and in Christ as the head of his body. The priest stands forth again as essentially ministerial and not as remote and cultic. The ministries of presbyter and bishop flow from the ministry of the apostles precisely as active ministers announcing the gospel and founding churches. The priest was no longer an isolated figure, ontologically different through the act of consecrating the Eucharist in a church where there were no other ministries, but the priest was the leader of a community, of a ministry of ministers, of a liturgy of participation.

After Vatican II, the centrist (and usually authoritarian) authority of the post-Reformation Catholic leader—pope, bishop, pastor—was complemented by formal and informal groups: international synods, Vatican commissions, national bishops conferences, priests associations, parish councils, advisory boards, conferences of superiors of religious orders, finance boards, etc.

The liturgy became public, active, intelligible, and varied. Theology escaped and expanded—escaped the dominance of apologetics and methods of meditation and expanded in the study of Scripture, knowledge of the history of theologies with a rediscovery of Origen or Aquinas in their contexts, creative systematic theologies, countless schools and institutes, new publishing houses and journals. Already in 1970, Yves Congar wrote perceptively: "It is astonishing how the postconciliar period has so little to do with the Council....While

---

4. Henri Denis, "La Théologie du presbyterat de Trente à Vatican II," *Les Prêtres* (Paris: Cerf, 1968), pp. 193-201; see O'Meara, "The Ministry of Presbyter and the Many Ministries in the Church," in Donald Goergen ed., *The Theology of Priesthood* (Collegeville: Liturgical Press, 2000), pp. 67-86.

'aggiornamento' means changes and adaptations to a new situation, assuming the principles of the original institution, the postconciliar questions are new and radical."[5]

Restoration

In the last ten years, at least, of this pontificate, Pope John Paul II has partly become a restorationist of the Baroque. He came to Rome from a church and a nation cut off from Europe for most of the twentieth century (and where the conciliar documents themselves were not in full translation until the 1980s).[6] The pope sees his experience as the standard for the entire Church: past, present, and future, East and West, but his experience of Church is the product of a Baroque Polish Catholicism from around 1920. There is an intent to draw all power back to the papacy to control theology in favor of papal statements and personal spirituality. The papal trips are pilgrimages, an activity so popular from 1800 to 1960. In the papal canonizations and beatifications (over 450) we see the Baroque honoring of men and women who are priests and nuns who lived in the seventeenth to early twentieth centuries. There is also the theology from around World War I that divides simplistically the gospel and the world. The style and externals of the new "religious movements" enclose a mechanics of clothes and rituals from the recent past, capes and sashes from the congregations of the

---

5. Congar, Private Letter of 12. 9. 1970.

6. Documents attempt to disguise this; the letter *Tertio Millenio Adveniente* says that Vatican II brought "a new era" but says that Catholics have yet to find the meaning or impact of the Council: "In the universal Church and in the particular churches, is the ecclesiology of communion described in *Lumen Gentium* being strengthened? Does it leave room for charisms, ministries, and different forms of participation by the People of God, without adopting notions borrowed from democracy and sociology which do not reflect the Catholic vision of the Church, and the authentic spirit of Vatican II?" The pope himself missed the postconciliar era and generally ignores it. The text speaks of "sensitivity to what the Spirit is saying to the churches…to individuals through charisms meant to serve the whole community," but his politics represses local episcopacies and ignores the expansion of lay ecclesial ministry. *Tertio Millenio Adveniente* 18, 20, 23 (36).

nineteenth century.[7] The Baroque held a theology of priestly dignity in a physical and metaphysical way, a lasting divine presence apart from the success of ministry. New liturgical alterations serve the physical separation of priests from baptized Catholics as though the second group were secular. The emphasis upon physical or metaphysical priestly distinctness, apart from ministerial success and social normality, has been an important cause of the situation joining sexual abuse to financial mismanagement. Whatever restoration is taking place is necessarily one of what people over sixty have experienced—it is the Baroque as altered in the nineteenth century. For a very few young people (usually marked by anxiety), it can be only a "curiosity shop" where one sees Christianity as "neat stuff."

A restoration is usually afraid of the ambiguity of preaching the gospel in a pluralistic world, afraid of complex difficulties facing the work of church life and ministry today. For instance, one can legalize when a Eucharistic minister receives Communion, but the revolution is that the baptized distribute Communion; one can issue an encyclical confusing and bemoaning aspects of ecumenism, but intra-church dialogues, church meetings, and theological conventions, lectures at seminaries of all churches, the reading of the great ecumenists continue around the world. The new religious movements are numerically tiny; it is not clear they will survive the support of this pontificate and wealthy American reactionaries; a few are already beginning to come to an end. Regardless, one cannot restore a culture or a church; the attempt to do so ends in acting out a play or a ballet. Commenting on times of change, C. S. Lewis once observed that the period people consider to be full of antiquity is usually the one just before their own.

---

7. Cardinal Ratzinger spoke of the movements' sectarian challenge to episcopal authority as "a childhood disease…tendencies to exclusivity and onesidedness, frictions." ("The Theological Locus of Ecclesial Movements," *Communio* 25 [1998], p. 481).

Conclusion

Catholicism is never living in only one period, is never fully engaged by the present epoch or represented solely by one "golden age." The ages intertwine. The Baroque inevitably continues on in Catholicism, because the sacramental notions from the Baroque—the forms of grace-in-nature making real and vivid Catholic truth in spirituality and art—continues on. The Baroque, however, cannot monopolize, cannot be very present.

What suggestions should be made?

- We should appreciate the lasting contribution of the Baroque, its lasting influence, the modern subjectivity of Ignatius and Teresa of Avila, the successful interplay of art and religion in that time, and of spirituality for the modern person, things needed in every age.
- We should work to see that theological reflection, pondering how a parish or diocese can be more vital, or discussing war and peace continues and expands. Thinking of Christianity and theology are not solely the responsibility of Rome and are not done well by Vatican employees. The richness of twenty centuries of theology should not be collapsed into platitudes and pious thought imposed according to obedience.
- We should recognize that, in America, faith is joined to some mature understanding of important issues. There may be no "simple Catholics" if there ever were any. It is important for preachers and teachers to be able to explain theologically the role of church authorities and the roles of others in the decision-making concerning new moral issues, to explain the eucharistic real presence and the centrality of Jesus in a world where grace is present in other religions.[8]
- We should support the bishops and the bishops' conferences in their search for a legitimate independence for their regional,

---

8. "What a Bishop Might Want to Know," *Worship* 68 (1994), pp. 55-63.

national, and local churches. Let them guide the Church freely, in thinking and serving.

- We should support the reality of expanded ministry in the Church, of ecclesial lay ministers—thirty-five thousand are currently preparing themselves for baptismal service—even as one supports drawing priests to parish leadership. One must recognize that the model of haves and have-nots—of exalted clergy and passive laity—has been replaced by a picture of a parish where concentric circles of ministry around leadership is active.

Time, Saint Augustine once said, never takes a holiday. It ticks away. The temptation to push time aside, to remain in some world of the past, to live apart from life, ultimately, leads to a backwater in which there is not much life. The Holy Spirit wants the Church on earth to take some new directions. Time and history are not fearful or hostile. They too are the creation of God. And, as Thomas Aquinas said, "Time itself can be our coworker."[9]

9. Thomas Aquinas, *Commentary on the* Ethics *of Aristotle,* bk. 4, l. 6; see Charles E. Curran, "Two Traditions. Historical Consciousness Meets the Immutable," *Commonweal* (October 11, 1986), p. 13; Heinrich Fries, "Wandel des Kirchenbildes und dogmatischer Entfaltung," *Mysterium Salutis* IV/I (Freiburg: Herder, 1967), pp. 223-289.

5. What Can We Learn From the Church in the Nineteenth Century?

Rev. Michael J. Himes, Boston College

What can we learn from the Church in the nineteenth century that will assist us in responding to the enormous challenges that we face in the Church in the twenty-first century? I offer a general observation followed by three points, each of which will lead me to a suggestion.

My general observation begins precisely where my colleague Father Thomas O'Meara concluded: the importance of history in understanding the Church's life and mission. This may be so self-evident to us at the beginning of the twenty-first century that we can fail to appreciate how revolutionary the idea was for many people in the nineteenth century. In 1845, the year of his reception into the Roman Catholic Church, John Henry Newman, until then an Anglican priest and a teacher at Oxford University, wrote his enormously important and influential *An Essay on the Development of Christian Doctrine*. I must caution those not familiar with the book not to be misled by the word "essay" in the title, which may suggest a piece the length of a magazine article. By calling his work an "essay," Newman meant that his lengthy book was an attempt to deal with a complex subject. He himself described it as "a hypothesis in solution of a difficulty." He intended his readers to take that description seriously: he was offering a hypothesis, a suggestion designed to explain a difficulty. But what is the difficulty? That, I think, is often misunderstood by readers of Newman's book today. Many readers, approaching the book for the first time, assume that he is offering a theory about how doctrine develops, and he does indeed offer some interesting comments about such a theory. That is not what the book is about, however.

The suggestion that Newman advances and that he requires hundreds of pages to support is not *how* doctrine develops but *that* doctrine develops. The very idea that doctrine could possibly develop over time was so foreign to Newman's contemporaries that he had to advance a very elaborate and detailed argument simply to support the possibility that it could happen before he could begin to consider about how it might be explained. Newman's problem, the difficulty he was trying to resolve, was something obvious but often overlooked. If someone in the nineteenth century looked about him or herself, he or she would have found many communities describing themselves as the Church of Jesus Christ. If such a person opened the pages of the New Testament, he or she would have found in the Acts of the Apostles, in the letters of Paul and the other letters of Christian writers of the New Testament, a description, explicit or implicit, of the Church of Jesus Christ. But the inquirer would have been forced to recognize that none of the churches that he or she saw in the nineteenth century looked like the one described in the New Testament. How are we to explain that discrepancy? Newman noted that three explanations had been advanced, all of which he found unsatisfactory, thus leading him to advance his own hypothesis.

The first position that he examined and found wanting was that, in fact, there never has been any change in the Church or in its teaching. Of course, various private opinions, ideas, and practices—some helpful, some heretical—have grown up among theologians and church leaders at different times and places. One had to distinguish ecclesial doctrine, however, which has always and everywhere remained the same, from these private opinions which come and go within the Church's life and may be more or less helpful. This position Newman described as, in his time, the typically Anglican hypothesis.

The second possible explanation for the apparent disparity between the Christian communities found in the New Testament and the churches that presently exist was that, early on, as early as the third or fourth generation of the Christian movement, Christian life and doctrine had been corrupted. Christian doctrine had been corrupted by taking over ideas and categories from Neoplatonism and other Greek philosophical schools, as well as from various mystery religions that arose in the ancient Near East just before and after the appearance of Christianity. The task of Christians today must be to discard all those accretions that have accumulated over the course of centuries, accretions which are, in fact, distortions, and so to get back to pure Christian doctrine. This was the radically Protestant hypothesis, as Newman understood it.

The third of the three inadequate hypotheses was characteristically held by Catholics, according to Newman. It explained the difference between the churches of the New Testament era and the current community by invoking the notion of the *disciplina arcani*, the "discipline of the secret." It is true that in the early Church certain teachings and practices were so revered, so sacred, so holy, that they were not disclosed to anyone and everyone indiscriminately. A person had to be ready to be committed to the community or already baptized before being instructed in these teachings or introduced into these practices. (For example, in some ancient churches, the Lord's Prayer, since it had been taught by Jesus to his disciples, was reserved for the baptized.) This principle of the *disciplina arcani* was invoked by some to explain what seemed to be changes in Church doctrine and life. Such changes were, indeed, simply a matter of appearance for everything the Church teaches now has always been part of its belief and practice. Not everything that Christians believed had been recorded and made public because some elements were so sacred that they had to be kept secret. In fact, bizarre as this may sound to us, one of the most distinguished figures of the French baroque church, and one of the great lights of seventeenth-century French literature—the Fulton Sheen of the late 1600s in France—Archbishop Jacques Bénigne Bossuet had actually maintained that everything decreed at the Council of Trent had been known to the twelve apostles, although they had not publicly taught them. Newman regarded this as the typically Catholic way of dealing with the difficulty.

None of these three attempts to explain the differences between the primitive and contemporary churches were satisfactory in Newman's judgment, and that was why he advanced his new hypothesis: Christian doctrine changes and develops over time. There has been real growth in the Church's doctrine, worship, and understanding of its own deepest mission. Newman's goal was not to explain how that development took place, merely that it had happened. That seems so evident to us that it may seem absurd to have to argue for the fact. But a review of Newman's book written in this country by a new convert to Catholicism from Unitarianism who was to become a very distinguished figure in the history of American Roman Catholic thought, Orestes Brownson, insisted, "The Church asserts that there has been no progress, no increase, no variation of faith, no change, that what she believes and teaches now is precisely what she has always and everywhere believed and taught from the first." Brownson then addressed Newman directly in the review: "If you believe the Church, you cannot assert development. If you do not believe her, you have no right to call yourself Catholic." Strong language, and an indication of how radical the mere suggestion of development and change in the Church's life and teaching was a mere one hundred and sixty years ago to most of the Catholic community.

Thus far my general observation. Now, to the first of my three points.

~

Earlier, Father Michael Buckley advocated the abolition of the role of papal nuncio as an ambassador of the Holy See to a particular country. The office of nuncio understood in this way is a nineteenth-century product. There has long been a Vatican diplomatic corps, of course, but the reason for its existence was the Papal States. We should remember that, until the middle of the nineteenth century, the central part of the Italian peninsula was an independent state directly ruled by the bishop of Rome, the pope. Thus, initially, papal nuncios were the ambassadors of the head of the Papal State accredited to other governments, just as the United States and Mexico exchange ambassadors. The papal nuncio, therefore, was not the representative of the head of the Church but rather the ambassador of the government of a portion of central Italy. Thus an exchange of diplomatic representatives between the Papal State and non-Catholic countries was possible, since the nuncio represented the head of a government, not the head of the Church. The changed status of the Vatican diplomatic corps is closely connected with the centralization of authority in the Holy See in the nineteenth century. Oddly enough, one of the unintentional architects of that centralization was Napoleon.

On July 12, 1790, a year into the French Revolution, the Constituent Assembly, at that point the governing body of France, passed the Civil Constitution of the Clergy, a rearrangement of the dioceses of France as well as a new procedure for appointing and paying bishops and pastors. According to the Civil Constitution, all bishops and pastors would be salaried employees of the French Republic. The administration of the Church was ultimately the responsibility of the French revolutionary government; the papacy's role was limited to doctrinal oversight. The French bishops objected to this, the Holy See understandably had grave reservations, and the French government entered into negotiations with the Vatican. Before those negotiations were completed (and it would have been interesting to see what would have happened had they been completed since there is some indication that Rome might possibly have been willing to accept part of what the Civil Constitution demanded), the Constituent Assembly acted on its own: on November 27, 1790, the Assembly passed the requirement of an oath of allegiance to the Civil Constitution of the Clergy. Thus all priests and bishops were forced to swear an oath, pledging their loyalty to the Civil Constitution. Pope Pius VI responded by condemning both the Constitution and the oath of allegiance on April 13, 1791. Many French priests and bishops refused to take the oath. They were deprived of their offices; some were arrested, and more fled the country. Some of those who remained in France were subsequently arrested and guillotined. But some French priests decided that in the midst of the turmoil in France it would be wrong to leave their people without pastors to celebrate Eucharist, baptize children, preside at weddings, and give Christian burial. If an oath of loyalty to the Civil Constitution of the Clergy would permit them to continue serving their people's needs in such confusing and dangerous times, they would take the oath, whether or not they were enthusiastic about the church order the Civil Constitution attempted to impose. In this way, good and devoted churchmen ended up on both sides of the issue—some bravely rejecting the oath and either going into exile or suffering the consequences in France, others swallowing their dismay at the oath and ministering to their flocks. Unsurprisingly, as the revolution degenerated into the Reign of Terror, as revolutionary positions became more fanatical, as executions and massacres mounted, great animosity developed between the clergy who took the oath and those who refused it. On the one hand, those who swore the oath and continued their pastoral work were regarded as traitors and schismatics by those who had had to flee the country; on the other hand, those clergy who had rejected the Civil Constitution of the Clergy and the oath of loyalty and fled the country were seen as living safely in England or Holland or Germany or Spain while leaving others to bear the burdens and face the dangers of ministry in the chaos at home. One side regarded themselves as the people who bore the heat of the day and stayed in the trenches, as it were; the other side saw themselves as martyrs for the truth, enduring exile rather than succumbing to the tyranny of the state.

In 1799, when Napoleon seized power and had himself declared First Consul for life, he very much wanted to secure the backing of the church for his new regime. The question was, "Which church?"— the church that had sworn allegiance to the Civil Constitution or the church that had refused to swear the oath, both of which were led by clergy who had acted in good conscience for understandable reasons and who now bitterly opposed one another. Which church was Napoleon to deal with? With typical brusqueness, Napoleon dealt with the issue by sweeping it off the table. He decided to deal with neither set of clergy. Instead, he determined to deal over the heads of both hierarchies, those who had taken the oath and those who had rejected it, and make his arrangement with the pope. So

Napoleon negotiated a concordat between his government and the Holy See, consulting neither the juring or nonjuring clergy in France. This established the precedent that the Holy See followed for all subsequent concordats. If a formal agreement were to be made between a civil government and the Church regarding the organization of the church within a country, the agreement would not be negotiated between the government and the leaders of the church in the country, i.e., not with the bishops or metropolitan bishops of the country, but with the Holy See.

Consequently, the legates of the Holy See no longer primarily represent the pope as head of the Papal State or even of its much diminished remnant, Vatican City, but as the head of the Church to the local government. I suggest that this is a bad precedent. It may have served Napoleon well but if it ever served the Church well, it does so no longer. It certainly makes perfect sense that on an international level (for example, at the United Nations) the Church have a voice and that it be the voice of the Holy See. But if the government of the United States needs to address the Church in the United States, or if the Church in the United States feels obliged to address its government, the bishops of the United States should speak for the Church, not the Holy See. The notion that the papal nuncio speaks for the Church to the government undercuts the pastoral role of the bishops.

~

In the nineteenth century, the Catholic theological faculty at the University of Tübingen emerged as one of the most creative and important centers of Catholic thought. Indeed, its influence has continued to the present. (Among others, Cardinal Walter Kasper is a distinguished representative of the Tübingen school.) The person often described as "the Father of the Catholic Tübingen school" is Johann Sebastian Drey, and certainly he set the tone and direction of much the work associated with that faculty in the last two hundred years. Drey offered a very different way of understanding theology from what was the usual norm in his time. Drey insisted that theology should not be understood as the study of propositional truths. The doctrines of the Church are not a set of statements on which theologians work in order to extract further understanding from them. Rather, Drey claimed, theologians study the concrete life of the Christian community; the Church is "the true basis of all theological knowledge," and it is through the life of the community that theology is prevented from dissolving "into airy, unsubstantiated speculation." Drey gave a remarkable analogy: "The Church is for the theologian what the state is for the political scientist, what the animal organism is for medicine: the concrete expression of the science itself, that through which it becomes positive."[1] As for a biologist the living organism is the subject of study, so for a theologian the living body of Christ is the subject of study. The Church, as Drey pointed out, is the community of all the baptized. Thus the lived experience of all the members of the Christian community is the source and norm of theology. Attention must, therefore, be paid to what Drey described as "an analogy to what within the state is called public opinion."[2] I think that what Drey described as analogous to public opinion was what John Henry Newman meant by the *sensus* or *consensus fidelium*, the "sense of the faithful."

Newman described the sense of the faithful in a famous 1859 essay, "On Consulting the Faithful in Matters of Doctrine." He suggested that one could think about the sense of the faithful in five ways: a testimony to the fact of apostolic dogma; as a sort of instinct or *phronema*, a Greek term which we might best translate as "fundamental intentionality," deep in the life of the Church; as an action of the Holy Spirit; as an answer to the Church's constant prayer; and as "a jealousy of error," by which he meant a sensitivity to whether something fits or clashes with the lived experience of the community. This latter point is illustrated by the fact that often in the Church we may not know how to say rightly what we believe, but we certainly recognize when it is said wrongly. So we may not be able to

---

1. *Brief Introduction to the Study of Theology*, 54.
2. Ibid., 342.

explain precisely what we mean when we say there are three persons in God, but if someone were to maintain that it means that there are three Gods, we would immediately respond that such a position is false. This jealousy of error—the ability to recognize an inadequate formulation of the Church's faith, this *phronema*—this basic direction of life and thought in the community, is the *sensus fidelium* that Newman regarded as absolutely central to the life of the Church. This continuing infallible presence of the Spirit guiding the life of the Church is the real gift of infallibility in the Church. That was why Newman had little difficulty in accepting the teaching on papal infallibility of Vatican I, although he thought that it was ill-timed and not especially well stated in the council's formulation. Vatican I, in its definition of papal infallibility, defines that, under certain conditions, the bishop of Rome is endowed with that infallibility with which Christ willed that his Church be endowed. So infallibility is not a personal possession of the bishops of Rome. Rather, they possess the charism of infallibility because they speak in the name of the Church, the whole people of God, which is the primary recipient of the charism.

Newman's description may sound unobjectionable to us, but it was a source of bitter controversy in 1859. Let me quote to you a notorious letter of Msgr. George Talbot, the highest-ranking English-speaking member of the Roman curia at the time. Writing of Newman's preposterous idea that one might consult the laity on matters of faith, Talbot asked, "What is the province of the laity?" He answered his own question: "To hunt, to shoot, and to entertain. These matters they understand, but to meddle with ecclesiastical matters they have no right at all."[3]

In the mid-nineteenth century, Newman's suggestion was

---

3. Apart from the outrageousness of limiting the laity's role to hunting, shooting, and entertaining, do not fail to note that the only lay people Talbot could even imagine were of a class wealthy enough to own large country houses where they could host shooting parties. It apparently never crossed his mind that Newman could possibly mean that the laity who mopped the floors in those country houses or the grooms who tended the horses in their stables should be consulted about matters of faith.

regarded as very radical, so radical indeed that Talbot described him as "the most dangerous man in England." I doubt that it appears so outrageous today. What is outrageous, however, is that we still have no clear and formally recognized ways of gauging the *sensus fidelium*. The documents of Vatican II and the 1983 Code of Canon Law refer to the need to consult the sense of the faithful. Yet we have no structure for reading the "public opinion" of the Church. If I may draw a comparison, we are all guaranteed by the Constitution of the United States that as citizens we have the right to vote freely. Imagine, however, that no polling places are ever established, no election days scheduled, and no ballots or voting machines provided. What does it mean to have a right if there is no structure by which the right can ever be exercised? What does it mean to speak of a *sensus fidelium* if no one can ever find out what it is? It is often said that the Church cannot make decisions or formulate its belief by a head count or a show of hands, that faith is not determined by opinion polls. I fully agree. But if the sense of the faithful is a necessary element in the Church's belief and practice, how is that sense consulted? I readily grant that polls and votes may not be the way to read the consensus of believers, but what is the way? Clearly it will not do to affirm the existence and importance of the *sensus fidelium* and then conclude that no one can read it at any given moment. To use Drey's analogy, one cannot assert both the importance of "public opinion" in the Church and the impossibility of ever knowing what it is. The great American philosopher William James maintained that, if something is true, it makes a difference, and if it makes no difference, it is not true. If it is true that there is a *sensus fidelium*, then it must make a difference; if it never makes a difference, then it is simply not true. We need to have some sort of formal, i.e., canonical, structure by which the sense of the faithful may be regularly consulted.

～

Johann Adam Möhler, a great nineteenth-century theologian who was first a student and later a colleague of Johann Sebastian Drey's at Tübingen, in his *Symbolics*, one of the most widely read theological texts of that century, wrote that "it is acknowledged that, resulting in part from the change of time and the abuses of the Church and effected in part by the inner process of conceptual development advanced by the method of contradictions, two systems governing the relationship between the pope and the bishops gained prevalence, the episcopal and the papal systems; the latter, without denying the divine institution of bishops, emphasized especially the power of the center while the former, without gainsaying the divine foundation of the primacy, sought especially to draw power toward the periphery. Because each acknowledges the divine nature of the other, they provided very useful antitheses in the Church's life so that through their counterbalancing action not only has free development proper to the parts been preserved but their union in an unbreakable and living whole has also been maintained."[4] Notice that Möhler suggests that in the life of the Church there is something like a system of checks and balances. Unlike the United States Constitution, with its threefold separation of powers, in the Church there are two balancing principles: a papal principle divinely instituted and necessary for the life of the Church, and an episcopal principle also divinely instituted and necessary for the life of the Church, and the tension between them keeps the Church alive and growing.

Turning yet again to John Henry Newman, we find him maintaining much the same thing, although he frames it in a characteristically odd and striking way. As Newman entered his seventy-sixth year, he became increasingly concerned about a work he had written forty years earlier while still an Anglican, entitled *Lectures on the Prophetical Office of the Church* which had been incorporated into a larger book, *The Via Media of the Anglican Church*. In this book, he had argued that the Church of England had maintained a middle course, a *via media*, between the continental Protestant churches which had discarded too much authentic Christian teaching and ritual at the time of the Reformation and the Roman Catholic Church which had allowed too many foreign accretions and superstitious

---

4. Symbolics, 43.

practices to creep into its tradition. Forty years after its first appearance, it remained his most widely read book among Anglicans. Newman was concerned that the stringent criticisms of Roman Catholicism that he leveled in *The Via Media of the Anglican Church* were unjust or, at least, inaccurate. His problem was that, in his midseventies, with poor eyesight and in failing health, he doubted that he would have the time or strength to write a lengthy correction. So he did something truly astonishing: he issued a new edition of his book of forty years before with a new one-hundred-page preface in which he attacked the very book it served to introduce. After carefully correcting what he thought was mistaken or exaggerated in his description of Catholicism in the first edition, he set out to offer a description of the Catholic Church as he had come to know it after living within it for thirty years.

Newman bases his description of the life of the Church on the familiar notion of Christ as fulfilling three roles or offices: priest, prophet, and king. As the Church continues the work of the Lord in the world, it too has these three responsibilities. The priestly office is essentially the task of fostering holiness, the building up of the spiritual life in individuals and communities. Its locus of operation, Newman maintains, is the local church, by which he means not only the parish or the diocese but the domestic church, the family, one's circle of friends and fellow-workers. These are the spheres in which we learn and practice holiness. After all, for most of us the first teachers of prayer were not pastors or bishops or catechists, but our parents. Our families and friends and neighbors introduced us to the practical life of faith, and it is in these circles that the priestly office of the Church is primarily exercised. Attention to the priestly office of the Church without corresponding attention to the prophetic and royal offices has a characteristic danger—"superstition and enthusiasm"—by which Newman seems to mean emotional extremism.

The Church's prophetic office is its teaching role, the responsibility of seeking to understand the gospel and trying to apply it in new ways in new situations. The first surprise in Newman's description is the locus of this prophetic office in the Church. It is exercised, Newman states, primarily in what he calls "the theological schools." The present-day reader may have expected him to place the teaching office in the hierarchy because we have become accustomed to thinking of the pope and bishops as *the* magisterium. But Newman observes that most bishops are so occupied with administrative responsibilities that it is unrealistic to expect them to be able to devote the necessary time and energy to biblical, theological, and historical scholarship. Popes and bishops themselves turn to theological consultants who are expected to have the requisite knowledge and expertise. So, in practice, the theological schools and faculties are the locus of the teaching or prophetic office in the Church, according to Newman. This office, too, can be destructive if exercised apart from the other two offices; if left too entirely to itself it leads to arid "rationalism."

The kingly office is the governing role, the responsibility of holding the body of Christ together and seeing to its well-being. Newman identifies this as the role of the pope and the bishops. This is the political task within the Church, understood in the classic sense of "politics" as the fostering of communities that make an authentically good life possible for their members. It, too, becomes destructive if pursued apart from the priestly and prophetic offices, for it leads to "ambition and tyranny."

What must not be overlooked in Newman's remarkable preface to the second edition of *The Via Media of the Anglican Church* is that he presumes that these three offices that the Church possesses will not always function easily together. Indeed, they often clash, compete, or form uneasy alliances of two offices against the third.[5] The Church flourishes when the three offices mutually check and balance one another, for in doing so they prevent the characteristic disadvantages that arise when any one of them is exclusively cultivated. He seems to suggest that when the three offices appear to function in perfect synchronicity it is often because one or a combination of

---

5. Newman thought that in his time the priestly and royal offices tended to cooperate in crushing the prophetic office.

two have begun to dominate the life of the Church. The Church is healthiest and works best when there is a certain mutual tension between the priestly, prophetic, and kingly offices. Indeed, in the final paragraph of the preface to the new edition of *The Via Media of the Anglican Church*, Newman writes: "Whatever is great refuses to be reduced to human rule, and to be made consistent in its many aspects with itself."[6] Communities that are great, that are living, never function with perfect smoothness and consistency. When we seek something that runs with the smoothness and precision of a well-oiled machine, we get precisely that—a machine, not a living community. A church that functions perfectly will not be great and living; it will be small and dead. Although he was describing the life of the Church in broader terms than Möhler—who intended his papal and episcopal principles as tendencies within only one of the three "offices," the kingly—Newman is clearly in agreement with the great Tübingen theologian who held that balancing principles are "very useful antitheses in the Church's life" because "through their counterbalancing action not only has free development proper to the parts been preserved but their union in an unbreakable and living whole has also been maintained."

In order to maintain that healthy tension between necessary roles and principles in the Church, I conclude by offering three suggestions corresponding to my three points drawn from the experience of the Church in the nineteenth century.

First, the Holy See must represent the Church in an international forum such as the United Nations. The usual spokespersons for the Church in any particular country to the government of that country ought rightly to be the national conference of bishops of the country. The authority of national episcopal conferences needs to be strengthened, not undermined.

Second, it is not enough to assert that the faithful have a right and even a duty to make known their opinions on matters affecting the Church's well-being, as canon law does, in fact,

---

6. *The Via Media of the Anglican Church*, paragraph 36.

assert.[7] Structures must be devised on every level of the Church's life—parochial, diocesan, national, and universal—by which public opinion in the Church can be heard and the *sensus fidelium* can be consulted on a regular basis, and these structures must be incorporated into canon law.

Third, at the present time, the centralization of executive and teaching authority in the Holy See is unprecedented in the history of the Church. The counterbalancing episcopal principle must be reasserted. This requires (a) creation of a different system for selecting bishops, (b) an international synod of bishops which will meet on a regular basis with the pope in sessions the agenda for which is not determined by the Roman curia and the conclusions of which are not written by the pope, and (c) greater authority for national episcopal conferences in cooperation with a national forum for the laity. These must be incorporated into canon law.

In conclusion, permit me to suggest to you that what you are part of today is not only a conference on history. The very fact that we are having such a conference *is history*. I compliment us all on being part of it. Drey and Möhler and Newman would have been very proud of us.

---

7. Canon 212, #3.

6. What Can We Learn From Vatican II?

Dr. Richard R. Gaillardetz, University of Toledo

I was a bit daunted when I was given my assignment by Fr. Himes. How could anyone possibly do justice to such an epochal event as Vatican II in a mere thirty minutes? Then I saw that Professor Harrington was assigned the whole New Testament and Professor Buckley the entire first millennium, so how could I complain!

The temptation for me is to summarize the teaching of the council and then say, "Here, go and make this teaching a reality." Indeed, there is so much still left for us to do in realizing the vision of the council set forward in its sixteen documents. Its teaching on the positive role of the laity, the important work of ecumenism, the need for renewal of the liturgy, the Church's mission to be a leaven in the world—these teachings, and so many more, are still in need of a fuller implementation in the life of the Church.

However, as committed as I am to furthering the teaching of the council, my inclination today is to adopt an alternative approach. I would like to discuss Vatican II as an ecclesial event, and explore what happened at Vatican II that might be instructive for us today. To do that, however, means that we spend a few moments contemplating the often overlooked fact that Vatican II might well have been played out in a very different way. A mere month before the council opened, Cardinal Giovanni Baptista Montini, the cardinal archbishop of Milan, sought a private audience with Pope John XXIII to warn him that he foresaw a disaster in the upcoming council. Cardinal Paul-Emile Léger, Cardinal Archbishop of Montreal, drafted an extensive twelve page letter which he sent to the pope on September 11, 1962, with the accompanying signatures of Cardinals Frings, Liénart, Döpfner, Suenens, and König.[1] In that letter, he warned that any hopes for real Church reform had been hijacked by those who

---

1. The letter is discussed in in Gilles Routhier, "Les réactions du cardinal Léger à la préparation de Vatican II," *Revue d'Histoire de l'Eglise de France* 80 (1994): pp. 281-302.

had been responsible for much of the planning of the council. Why were these bishops so fearful that the council would fail?

Preparations for the Council: Stacking the Deck

Pope John XXIII's announcement of an upcoming council marked the beginning of over three years of preparation for the council. There was little in this preparation that augured well for substantive reform of the Church.

The Ante-preparatory Commission

An ante-preparatory commission had been established by Pope John under the presidency of Cardinal Tardini. The work of this commission would transpire in three phases: 1) soliciting initial proposals from curial officials, bishops, religious superiors (male only), university faculties, and theologians; 2) drawing up a rough outline of topics to be addressed based on the questionnaires; and 3) proposing membership for the various preparatory commissions. The membership of this commission was one of the main reasons why Vatican insiders were pessimistic of any real reform being accomplished. The commission was comprised primarily of the secretaries and other representatives from each of the Roman congregations, individuals hardly eager to undertake substantive Church reform.

The ante-preparatory commission sent out questionnaires to 2812 bishops, theologians, religious superiors (male only), theological faculties, and Roman congregations. Of this number, 2150 replied in some manner, though many were short and perfunctory. The commission then organized these responses into various categories of issues and questions that would need to be addressed by the soon-to-be appointed preparatory commission. Unfortunately, in the process of classification, the significance of many of the proposals was obscured by the fact that the material was classified according to the categories of canon law and the neo-scholastic manual tradition. Innovative proposals often as not fell through the cracks. More significant, however, was the fact that many of the curial officials on the commission found the very process of consultation distasteful. The notion of a consultation was seen as a slap at the curial leadership, and it smacked of a democratic mentality which had no place, they believed, in Christ's Church.

The lists of topics produced by the ante-preparatory commission were intended to guide the preparatory commissions in the drafting of council documents. However, the fragmentary and unfocused character of these reports helps explain why the preparatory schemata which emerged from the preparatory commissions lacked any common vision or sense of the overarching goal of the council.

The final task of the ante-preparatory commission was to propose membership to the ten (later eleven) preparatory commissions which would actually have the responsibility of drawing up draft documents to be given to the bishops for council debate. The pope then appointed the membership of the preparatory commissions based on these recommendations. This meant that, with a few noteworthy exceptions, the preparatory commissions were also placed in the hands of the leading curial officials least disposed to upset the ecclesial status quo.

Many leading bishops were dismayed at the way in which the deck was stacked in the appointments to the preparatory commissions. Cardinal Leo Suenens, in his memoirs writes:

> In the presence of the entire group [a special steering committee created by Pope John], I asked him: "Holy Father, why did you appoint the prefects of Roman Congregations to head the Council Commissions? This can only inhibit the freedom of Council members in their work and in their discussions." He answered, laughing: "...You're quite right, but I didn't have the courage."[2]

---

2. Leon-Joseph Cardinal Suenens, *Memories And Hopes* (Dublin: Veritas, 1992), p. 71.

Rules of the Council

Another of the tasks of the ante-preparatory commission was that of drawing up the rules of the council. In his very first press conference, Cardinal Tardini had announced that many bishops were concerned about being drawn away from their dioceses for an extended period of time. Consequently, the likely procedure would be to have preparatory texts drafted in advance of the council and then sent to the bishops for their comments. That way, when the bishops actually arrived at the council, they would be able to vote on an already revised text "reflecting their views." Later, Fr. Sebastian Tromp, secretary for the Theological Commission, would come to the defense of Tardini's view, to the point of arguing that it wasn't even necessary for the bishops to actually gather in one place! Tromp also noted the logistical problems of having as many as three thousand bishops gathered in one place. He further remarked, "There is a danger that it will be extremists who do most of the talking and that the voice of moderates will not be heard."[3] This was followed by Paul Phillippe, a representative of the Holy Office, who made the remarkable suggestion that the bishops need not be allowed to actually speak at the council, but only to offer written comments in advance and then simply cast their vote on the *schemata* at the general session. Fortunately, the views of Tromp and Philippe were quite extreme, and perhaps spurred other bishops and curialists to insist on the fundamental right of bishops to speak at a council.

The authority for determining the rules of the council was placed in the hands of the pope, following the model of Vatican I. In the summer of 1962, the pope promulgated the rules of procedure for the council as the *Ordo Concilii Oecumenici Vaticani II Celebrandi.*[4]

---

3. Quoted in Joseph Komonchak, "The Struggle for the Council During the Preparation of Vatican II (1960-1962) in *History of Vatican II,* edited by Giuseppe Alberigo and Joseph A. Komonchak (Maryknoll: Orbis, 1995), I: 327n.555.

4. *Acta et Documenta Concilio oecumenico Vaticano II apparando; Series prima (ante-preparatoria),* volume II Part I (Rome: Typis Polyglottis Vaticanis, 1960-61), p. 434. [Henceforward, ADP]

One of the more significant rules for the council determined that the council would be conducted in its entirety in Latin. There is some thought that this was intended to put the non-Italian bishops at a disadvantage, though early in the council it became readily apparent that many of the Italian prelates were not nearly as good at Latin as they had fancied themselves to be. Nevertheless, the language rule presented major difficulties because many of the bishops, particularly those indigenous bishops from the Third World who had little facility in Latin, would be hampered in conciliar discussions.

The rules of the council also stipulated that each council commission, successors to the preparatory commissions, were to be comprised of twenty-four bishops, two-thirds elected by the council and one-third appointed by the pope. This may seem reasonable until one realizes that at Vatican I *all* the members of conciliar commissions were elected by the assembly.

In general it can be said that the rules of the council were clearly formulated to maximize curial control of the conciliar proceedings. Joseph Komonchak observes:

> *Papally appointed preparatory commissions would provide the texts for conciliar discussion. Papally appointed presidents would direct its course, and a papally appointed secretary would expedite its administration. Papal appointees would chair the conciliar commissions, one-third of whose members would also be appointed by the pope.*[5]

As Komonchak also observed, these rules were clearly made for what was anticipated to be an unproblematic and non-controversial council whose agenda and texts would be prepared in advance and approved with little debate. Consequently, when significant disagreement regarding the schema occurred, the rules provided little concrete guidance.

---

5. Komonchak, "The Struggle for the Council...," pp. 333-4.

Draft Documents

The preparatory commission produced some seventy draft documents for conciliar consideration. Seven of them were sent to the bishops in advance of the opening of the council, but only in late August. In the minds of many, this was done in order to minimize the bishops' opportunity to gather theological critiques of the documents prior to the opening of the council.

No Plan for the Council

Another shocking feature of the conciliar preparations was the fact that there was, in the midst of all of the preparations for the council, no concrete plan for how the council would conduct its business, what documents it would address, and in which order. Cardinal Suenens had raised this issue with the pope in March of 1962. Suenens recalls querying the pope:

> *"Who is working on an overall plan for the Council?"*
> *"Nobody,"* said Pope John.
> *"But there will be total chaos. How do you imagine we can discuss seventy-two schemata…?"*
> *"Yes,"* John agreed, *"we need a plan….Would you like to do one?"*[6]

This was a rather delicate matter. The pope certainly agreed that an overall plan was needed, but he did not wish to appear as if he was imposing his will on the wishes of all the bishops. Consequently, the pope also asked Suenens to discuss his plans with Cardinals Montini, Döpfner, Siri, and Liénart. The pope directed Suenens: "Bring them together so that I will be able to say, 'According to the wishes of a number of cardinals,' while being a bit vague on the

---

6. This account is taken from Léon-Joseph Suenens, "A Plan for the Whole Council," in *Vatican II by Those Who Were There*, edited by Alberic Stacpoole (London: Chapman, 1985), pp. 88-91.

details. Then it won't just look like something I've cooked up."[7] With that, Suenens drafted a pastoral plan for the council that provided some important criteria for determining what the council should and should not address. He sent that draft on to Cardinal Cicognani, but then it seems to have been put in a drawer somewhere.

Commissions ill-disposed to reform, rules intended to marginalize all but curial officials, poor draft documents, the lack of a council plan—all these factors contributed to the low expectations for any substantive reform as the opening of the council approached. The question is, why, in spite of all of the signs suggesting disaster, did the council succeed in the reform of the Church?

Changing the Course of the Council

The first and most significant factor in redirecting the course of the council came from Pope John XXIII.

Pope John's Opening Address

On September 23, 1962, Pope John learned that he was suffering from cancer and would not have long to live. At the time, it was still thought that the entire business of the council might be concluded in one session. The council opened on October 11, 1962, with a Mass of the Holy Spirit. A few excerpts from this crucial address will help us appreciate how much the pope's own address set the ecclesial tone for the council:

> *Illuminated by the light of this council, the Church—we confidently trust—will become greater in spiritual riches and gaining the strength of new energies there from, she will look to the future without fear. In fact, by bringing herself up-to-date where required, and by the wise organization of mutual cooperation, the Church will make men and women, families and peoples really turn their minds to heavenly things....*

---

7. Recounted in Peter Hebblethwaite, *Paul VI: The First Modern Pope* (New York: Paulist, 1993), p. 301.

...We wish to narrate before this great assembly our assessment of the happy circumstances under which the ecumenical council commences. In the daily exercise of our pastoral office, we sometimes have to listen, much to our regret, to voices of persons who, though burning with zeal, are not endowed with too much sense of discretion and measure. In these modern times they can see nothing but prevarication and ruin. They say that our era, in comparison with past eras, is getting worse and they behave as though they learned nothing from history, which is, none the less, the teacher of life. They behave as though at the time of formal councils everything was a full triumph for the Christian idea and life and for proper religious liberty. We feel we must disagree with those prophets of gloom, who are always forecasting disaster, as though the end of the world was at hand. In the present order of things, Divine Providence is leading us to a new order of human relations which, by men and women's own efforts and even beyond their very expectations, are directed toward the fulfillment of God's superior and inscrutable designs....

The greatest concern of the ecumenical council is this: that the sacred deposit of Christian doctrine should be guarded and taught more efficaciously....In order, however, that this doctrine may influence the numerous fields of human activity, with reference to individuals, to families and to social life, it is necessary first of all that the Church should never depart from the sacred patrimony of truth received from the Fathers. But, at the same time, she must ever look to the present, to the new conditions and new forms of life introduced into the modern world which have opened new avenues to the Catholic apostolate....The salient point of this council is not, therefore, a discussion of one article or another of the fundamental doctrine of the Church which has repeatedly been taught by the Fathers and by ancient and modern theologians, and which is presumed to be well know and familiar to all. For this a council was not necessary. But...the Christian, Catholic, and

*apostolic spirit of the whole world expects a step forward to-
ward a doctrinal penetration and a formation of consciences
in faithful and perfect conformity to the authentic doctrine....
The substance of the ancient doctrine of the Deposit of Faith is
one thing, and the way in which it is presented is another....*

*We see...as one age succeeds another, that the opinions of
men and women follow one another and exclude each other.
And often errors vanish as quickly as they arise, like fog before
the sun. The Church has always opposed these errors. Frequently she has condemned them with the greatest severity.
Nowadays, however, the spouse of Christ prefers to make use
of the medicine of mercy rather than that of severity. She considers that she meets the needs of the present day by demon-
strating the validity of her teaching rather than by condem-
nations....*

*Unfortunately, the entire Christian family has not yet fully
attained to this visible unity in truth. The Catholic Church,
therefore, considers it her duty to work actively so that there
may be fulfilled the great mystery of that unity, which Jesus
Christ invoked with fervent prayer....*[8]

These passages set forth not so much an agenda as a new conciliar framework that would become a source of inspiration for the
bishops in the years ahead.

Determining the Membership
of the Conciliar Commissions

Yet another significant event in redirecting the course of the council
took place on the very first day of the first general congregation of
the council on October 13, 1962. The first order of business was the
election of bishops to the conciliar commissions, successors to the preparatory commissions. This was to be conducted under the presidency

---

8. Excerpts taken from the English translation in *The Documents of Vatican II*, ed., Walter
M. Abbott (New York: Crossroad, 1989), pp. 710-19.

of Cardinal Tisserant, a formidable, conservative curialist. A list of those bishops who served on the preparatory commissions was distributed among the council members with the clear expectation that these bishops would be reelected to the respective commissions. Had this occurred, it is difficult to know what course the council might have taken. However, a few weeks before the opening of the council, some of the leading European bishops had gotten wind of the plan to have the preparatory commission members reelected. They developed their own strategy. At the opening meeting, immediately upon the distribution of the list of candidates for the new commissions, Cardinal Liénart of Lille, primate of France, rose to speak. Cardinal Tisserant informed him that the rules did not permit an intervention at this point, but Liénart continued anyway and, without being formally recognized by the president of the assembly, moved that the election be postponed until the bishops could meet in regional caucuses in order to add their own nominations to the list of candidates. Cardinal Frings of Cologne then rose and seconded the motion. Before Tisserant could prevent further objection to this violation of procedures, their proposal was met with such an ovation that Tisserant conceded the point and the first session was adjourned after fifteen minutes! In that brief encounter, it became clear that this was not going to be a council content to rubber stamp curial documents.

Montini's Plan for the Council

During the first week of the council, Cardinal Montini (later Pope Paul VI) was beginning to panic that there was no plan for the council. He wrote a letter to Cardinal Cicognani, but which he knew would find the eyes of the pope. In that letter he expressed concern over the lack of any plan for the council. In essence he was asking why the Suenens plan was not being announced. Soon after, with Pope John's approval, Montini reworked Suenens' plan. He mapped out a detailed agenda for the council, which he envisioned, following Suenens, as consisting of three sessions (a fourth would eventually be necessary): the first being more doctrinal in character, the last two more pastoral. The pope was alarmed at the mention of more than one session, as he had desperately hoped to see the council through and he knew that, with the advance of his cancer, he was not likely to be alive for any further sessions. Nevertheless, he accepted the plan.

Removal of the Preparatory Schema on Divine Revelation

Immediately after debate began on the Schema on Divine Revelation during the first session of the council, a number of bishops rose in fundamental opposition to the schema. Among those who criticized the schema were Cardinals Liénart (Lille), Frings (Cologne), Léger (Montreal), Alfrink (Utrecht), Suenens (Malines), Ritter (St. Louis), and Bea. The schema was defended by the Italians Ottaviani, Ruffini (Palermo), and Siri (Genoa). The major point of contention regarded the two-source theory of revelation, that is, the theory then popular in many of the dogmatic manuals used in seminaries holding that there were two distinct sources of divine revelation, Scripture and tradition. As one might imagine, this formulation was very problematic for Protestants, and many Catholic theologians had insisted that this formulation departed from the ancient tradition of the Church. Liénart was adamant in his insistence on the rejection of this schema. He pointed out that the Church had never formally taught that there were two sources of revelation but rather one font, the Word of God, transmitted in different modes. Soon Frings and Alfrink joined Liénart in demanding the rejecting of the schema, as did Cardinal Ritter from St. Louis.

In response, Cardinal Ottaviani claimed that the rules of the council did not permit the complete rejection of a schema but only its modification. Finally the secretary general for the council, Archbishop Felici, called for a vote on the status of the schema. The explanation of the balloting offered by Cardinal Ruffini, however, was quite confusing and it is apparent that not a few council members were unsure as to the implications of their vote: 1368 voted for rejecting the schema, 822 for retaining it. Since the rules required a two-thirds majority, the schema was retained. The next morning, however, Pope John ordered that the schema be withdrawn and turned the matter over to a joint commission to be presided over by both Cardinal Ottaviani and the more progressive Cardinal Bea. The pope indicated that the new schema was to be short, irenic, and pastoral. The message the pope sent to the council was clear: This is *your* council.

The Education of the Episcopate

One of the more surprising sidelights of such an extended council was the opportunity that many bishops had, often for the first time since their seminary days, to take advantage of the recent developments in theology, biblical studies, and church history. The bishops would be in Rome, during each session, for several months. This gave them considerable opportunity to visit with one another and learn about the Church in various parts of the world. These meetings gave many bishops their first glimpse of the real diversity already existing within the Church. The extended time in Rome also provided bishops with the opportunity to attend evening lectures given by such eminent scholars as Karl Rahner, Piet Fransen, and Barnabas Ahern. So threatening was the influence of these theologians on the bishops that Cardinal Ottaviani petitioned John XXIII to have the Jesuits at the Biblical Institute cease giving lectures to groups of bishops. He also asked that Karl Rahner be asked to leave Rome. The pope asked who it was that was inviting these theologians to speak. When told that the bishops themselves had proffered the invitations, he said that he would not interfere in the legitimate right of bishops to become better informed regarding the questions being debated at the council.[9]

The well known Vaticanologist, Giancarlo Zizola, tells the story of visiting Bishop Albino Luciani (the future Pope John Paul I) during the council. He was staying at a Roman *pensione* run by some Italian sisters. Luciani admitted that he tried to spend each afternoon in his room studying, because, as he put it:

---

9. Xavier Rynne, *Vatican Council II* (one-volume edition, New York: Farrar, Straus and Giroux, 1999), p. 92.

...everything I learned at the Gregorian is useless now. I have to become a student again. Fortunately I have an African bishop as a neighbor in the bleachers in the council hall, who gives me the texts of the experts of the German bishops. That way I can better prepare myself.[10]

What all of this suggests is that part of the success of the council is due to the fact that the bishops, authoritative teachers of the faith, had the courage to become students once more.

What Can We Learn?

Having reviewed some of the factors that redirected the course of the council toward substantive reform, we can now ask what we might learn today from this account of the council.

Trusting Genuine Collegiality

One of the crucial reasons why Vatican II succeeded was Pope John XXIII's confidence in the bishops. Pope John did not, as best as we can tell, have a specific ecclesiological agenda. He trusted the insight of his bishops and intervened in the council whenever he felt their will was being thwarted by bureaucratic power plays. This trust in the work of the bishops is as important today as ever. Unfortunately, authentic episcopal collegiality is often frustrated by church structures and Vatican attitudes that remain resistant to the exercise of collegiality. World synods of bishops are carefully orchestrated by the Vatican and are conducted in a manner guaranteed to minimize genuine episcopal debate. The authority of episcopal conferences has been weakened by recent papal decrees. The Vatican attitude seems to be one which sees the bishops as executors of the will of the Vatican rather than as genuine collaborators with the bishop of Rome. In light of these difficulties, we might consider the following

---

10. Giancarlo Zizola, "He Answered Papal Summons to Journalism," *National Catholic Reporter* (October 4, 2002), p. 10.

proposal as one way to recover Pope John's confidence in the work of the bishops:

> Proposal 1: The creation of a permanent synod of bishops with deliberative and not merely consultative authority, crafted according to the model of the synods of the eastern churches, which would share responsibility with the pope for preserving the unity of faith and communion. One possibility would be to have a permanent synod comprised of all the metropolitan archbishops in the universal Church that would meet twice a year to deliberate with their head, the bishop of Rome, over matters of concern for the universal Church.

The council also called for substantive reform of the Roman curia. In its *Decree on the Bishops' Pastoral Office,* the council noted that the members of the curia were to "perform their duties in [the pope's] name and with his authority for the good of the churches and in the service of the sacred pastors" (CD # 9). Interestingly, in the revised Code of Canon Law, reference to serving the bishops was deleted. Many ecclesiologists and canon lawyers agree that there is a desperate need for a thoroughgoing reform of the Curia, as is reflected in the following proposal:

> Proposal 2: A major canonical reform of the curia is required to make it clearer that the curia serves the bishops and not the other way around. This reform should place much more explicit limits on when the curia can and cannot intervene in matters that do not clearly and directly threaten the unity of faith and communion of the universal Church. A concrete reform would more clearly tie the work of the curia to service of the permanent synod mentioned earlier, or, alternatively, to decentralize the curia, splitting it into regional bureaucratic offices more closely aligned with bishops conferences and subject to their authority.

Church Teachers Must be Willing to Learn

The bishops at the council were humble enough to believe that they had much to learn. They willingly entrusted themselves to the best of contemporary scholarship, regardless of ideology, and then exercised their proper role as pastors and guardians of the faith. When the International Theological Commission was created under Pope Paul VI, many hoped for new developments in theological consultation in which the Holy See and all the bishops would consult internationally respected theologians belonging to different schools of thought. The pope had envisioned that the commission would serve a consultative role, not only to the pope himself but to the Congregation for the Doctrine of the Faith. This important papal initiative must be expanded. A frequent consultation of theologians representing divergent views on a matter need not threaten the legitimate authority of those who hold church office. Unfortunately, in the last fifteen years the diversity of views represented by the ITC membership has diminished considerably, and some fear a return to the practice of limiting Vatican consultation to "court theologians." This concern leads to yet a third proposal:

Proposal 3: Revised structures for theological consultation at the local and universal levels. These structures, like the present International Theological Commission, must represent a genuine diversity of theological perspectives, and allow for legitimate and respectful dissent from authoritative, non-infallible teaching.

It is true that the Church today has much to learn from the teaching of Vatican II, and we must continue to work toward the dissemination of the teaching of the council. What I have proposed today, however, is that we can also learn much from the *conduct* of the council, from the pope's relationship to the bishops, the bishops' work with theologians, etc. The conduct of the council itself offers us a model for how the Church today can become a genuine community of corporate discernment led by its leaders to read the signs of the times and bring the gospel to bear on the questions of our age. If we are faithful to that task, perhaps we can fulfill the hope of Pope John XXIII, who once called for an ecclesial renewal that would restore "the simple and pure lines that the face of the Church of Jesus had at its birth."[11]

---

11. Rynne, p. 8.

Panel Discussion

Richard Miller: The life work of Bernard Lonergan, the very distinguished Canadian theologian, basically boiled down to the idea that "questions are our friends." In that light, I apologize that we won't be able to treat many of the questions forwarded today. All the questions were looked at and collated by a whole group of people, and I had to try to bring them to some synthesis to fit it into an hour and a half.

I'm going to begin with Fr. O'Meara's questions. Fr. O'Meara, you suggested, if I'm understanding this correctly, "that time is on our side" with regard to the current challenges of the Church. How do you feel that time is on our side? I think this question is getting at the issue of a certain impatience for change, and that there are serious challenges that need to be addressed. How do we, in light of the serious challenges that need to be addressed, talk about "time being on our side"?

Thomas O'Meara: Well, that's a very profound question. I think what the questioner might be thinking is that there's impatience and that there is a feeling that the Church has become static and without injections of new ideas. But that is not really "time." I would suggest that's the avoidance of time and hiding from it. The fact is that if we see things remaining from the restoration—those institutions that have been criticized today—I think that, as time goes on, we see that they cannot do the job, they can't be the Church or help the Church be the Church. We could rejoice if there were two or three times as many diocesan priests ordained, but that would not remove the fact that there are tens of thousands of the baptized in other ministries. We simply have moved beyond that situation, and I think that time, as well as the statistics mentioned in the opening of this symposium, call the Church and its leaders to be pastorally responsive. I don't think "the times" ever suggest that you hide.

Richard Miller: Since this day has been so concerned with the issue of time and change, would other speakers like to comment? Many of the questions suggest a sense that there are serious challenges and a certain impatience, shall we say, as well as the problem that if there isn't that impatience, then apathy can result. So how do you balance both realistic energy and life with the reality of patience?

Daniel Harrington: If I could speak for the field of Scripture, one of the great emphases of Vatican II was the importance of making Scripture the soul of theology, having it inform every part of Church life. And that takes time, it takes patience, and it also takes hard work. I think one of the important challenges for the future is to make us a more biblical Church. I think we need to study Scripture, to assimilate it as best we can, and—as I tried to illustrate this morning—learn from it. Over time, these long-term projects can often serve short-term concerns and solve short-term problems precisely because they come from spiritual depth. And I think the task of making our own Church more biblical is a long-term project that demands a lot of study and effort. My point is that we have to stick with it.

Michael Himes: I think time is on our side in the sense that you can't stand still. There is no possibility of saying "Well, we like things exactly as they are. We don't want anything to change." If you change nothing, its meaning will change. If you decide that you liked the way you dressed when you were seventeen—because you were right in the forefront of how seventeen-year-olds should dress—and you dress like that for the next fifty years, you won't be a stylish seventeen-year-old, you'll be a really weird sixty-seven-year-old. If you try to stand still, the world moves around you, and you aren't where you thought you were. My favorite description of the process of tradition is in *Through the Looking Glass*, the second of Lewis Carroll's *Alice* books, in which the Red Queen grabs Alice by the arm and says, "Quick, run!" and they start to run and run and run, and the Queen keeps saying, "Faster, faster, faster!" and Alice is almost ready to collapse, and finally the Queen says "Stop!" and Alice stops, collapses to the ground, and, as she looks around, she sees they are exactly where they were when they started. And Alice says, "But we didn't go anywhere!", to which the Queen says, "Ah, my dear, here you must run as fast as you can to stay where you are. If you want to go somewhere else, you must run twice as fast." And that's exactly the case with tradition: If you want to say what you always have said, you have got to change how you say it as quick as you can, because if you keep saying it the same way, it won't mean what it always meant.

Thomas O'Meara: That inspired me with another idea. I think time is on your side if you have a lot of people and a lot of ideas and a lot of energy and a lot of dedication, which the Catholic Church in America has had and does have. If you're the "Schwenkfelders,"[1] or a church where you don't have people in education, then time is not on your side because you're in the process of declining and dying. Time is on our side because the Catholic population increases and in that we presume we have all these people, all these institutions, many people going into theology, and people thinking and everything. In that sense, time will be on our side; but if you were to reach a point where you did not have the energy and the vitality that we once had, then time would turn against you.

Michael Buckley: The only person that Tolstoy unreservedly praises in *War and Peace* is General Kutusov. Everyone was pushing Kutusov to take on Napoleon as he marched into Russia, and Kutusov kept repeating, "You want Kiev, it's yours. You want Minsk, it's yours." He retreated ever farther because he was convinced that Napoleon eventually would destroy himself. The expression that Kutusov kept using, which is repeated almost like a mantra, is "patience and time, patience and time." This, however, is very delicate, because you could

---

1. A small Christian denomination in Southeastern Pennsylvania, named after Caspar Schwenkfeld von Ossig, who started a mass migration from Silesia to Pennsylvania in 1735.

have something that looks like patience which in fact is a delay in the reform of a particular institution. This is gradualism and a cop-out. On the other hand, you can have just the opposite. It's like screaming at an eighth-grade kid because he's not a senior in college. If you push too strongly on organic life, you destroy it. It reminds me of Saint Thomas Aquinas, quoting the Book of Proverbs: "It is very important to remember that he who blows his nose too vigorously draws blood." You can do a great deal of harm. There is no escape from the discernment about how one enters, in a reverent way, towards the things that you want to help, reform, while respecting its nature, so that it is not on the one hand gradualism and on the other hand a destructive kind of haste.

Richard Miller: Thank you very much. The next question is for the whole panel. That means that any of you can take it up. It doesn't mean that each of you has to address it. Is there any good that can come out of the present scandal in the American Church?

Catherine Mooney: I think probably so—it has all of us talking. I think that's a tremendous good. It has a conference like this taking place. Sometimes it takes a slap in the face to wake up and realize you might want to change something. As an historian, I bear in mind that this is not by any stretch of the imagination the worst thing that has happened in the history of the Church, even though sometimes it's made to be so. It *is* an awful thing that has happened, but we're human beings, we're going to continue to make mistakes, great mistakes, from time to time. The challenge is to respond to them with grace and a willingness to work hard, and I feel that is beginning to happen, not only in this country but in other places as well. Personally, I am very hopeful about the Church right now, hopeful that there are good members of the hierarchy who are looking at the situation, listening to laity, very hopeful about laity asserting themselves, realizing that the model of being passive listeners—that so many of us have been raised with—not only doesn't work, it's an abdication of our duty. So I find that tremendously hopeful.

Daniel Harrington: I preach every Sunday in two parishes in the Boston area and I work very hard at these homilies. I think it's important for me, who studies Scripture professionally and teaches people with strong theological educations, to be able to say these things to people who don't study Scripture continually and do not have theological educations. So it's a very important and challenging thing for me personally. Last September, after things had been unraveling in Boston for over six months, an elderly lady with all the goodwill in the world approached me and said: "Father, your sermons have gotten much better since the crisis." Well, I thought they were pretty good before, but this sort of underscores and makes concrete the point made by Cathy; it has us talking about these things, and we wouldn't have a meeting like we had today. So this can be (as I said at the beginning of my own talk, every crisis can be an opportunity) an opportunity to rethink some very important elements in our Church life.

Richard Miller: The next question is also for the whole panel. The issue really is about an informed laity. Given the fact that the laity is more educated than ever before, how do we deal with the issue of a theologically informed laity? That's one question. And then there are a few questions on how to deal with the seminary education in terms of how they perceive the laity.

Catherine Mooney: Let me just say something about the last part. I've been at Weston Jesuit School of Theology just two years, and it's been a wonderful experience. It's a Jesuit Theologate, where the Jesuits come for their last years of training before ordination. It's wonderful to work with these men who have good training and have a terrific commitment to the Church, and whom I think will be wonderful ministers. Another feature of the school is that it has many lay students, as well as members of other religious orders. I can't give you the exact percentage, but it's a very significant percentage of the students who are lay. They all study together, follow the same curriculum, and often participate in similar ministries. They do some collaborative ministerial projects. They are being trained to work together in harmony as a team. I think this is something that a lot of us don't know is going on in seminaries like Weston. This year, in particular, it dawned on me that the lay students were going to go out and work in parishes. I knew these students to be exemplary people, tremendously generous, and I thought to myself, "Gee, I've never been in a parish that has had a lay person who's quite so articulate and educated." I've had some excellent priests and some excellent sisters, and I thought this is a quiet thing that is happening, that some of these seminaries are putting people out there, and they're going to be working in parishes, and that's going to change the face of our parishes. It is a little bit like the first time we saw a woman reading Scripture at the podium or ministering at the altar. Now, it's not so surprising to have lay people who are every bit as articulate as some of the ministers and to have ordained ministers in parishes who have grown up with the idea of working with the laity. I think it's a quiet revolution that is slowly putting out some significant roots.

Richard Miller: Let me just follow up on that. Weston is a Jesuit school of theology. Can anyone speak on behalf of diocesan seminarian education? I think that would be Fr. Himes.

Michael Himes: For my sins, I was the dean of a seminary for ten years, and then I repented. At the present time, diocesan seminaries in the United States are a very mixed bag. There are some really excellent diocesan seminaries; there are some absolutely dreadful diocesan seminaries. Often, the dreadful ones are suffering from the fact that bishops are unwilling to close them. And they're simply too small to be viable. One of the things that I often have occasion to say to new students at Boston College is that there are three things that make a great university: a great faculty, a great library, and a great student body. The student body is the one aspect that most people forget, because, in fact, in the course of four years, they will all speak to one another much more than they are going to speak to me or any of my colleagues. And so, unless they're really interesting and intelligent people, for four years they're going to spend an awful lot of time in boring conversations. One of the things that's not often recognized is that education requires critical mass. There are schools that are just too small to be really excellent educational institutions. If you've got a seminary population of twenty or twenty-five, that's simply not a critical mass. That's not enough people to generate that kind of ongoing challenging, interesting, informative conversation which is what education has to be. I think there is a need for a *national* decision to be made about diocesan seminaries. It's not going to happen with individual bishops. The USCCB has got to end up saying we want ten diocesan seminaries in the United States—one in the Pacific Northwest, one in the Bay Area, one in the Southwest, one in the upper Midwest, etc.—and that we're going to close and/or merge seminaries to end up with really viable institutions. I really think that's a necessary step at the present time. I do not expect it to happen for next semester, but sooner or later, I think it has to happen.

Thomas O'Meara: I wanted to offer some observations from the point of view of college undergraduates. I notice that the rhetoric of Boston College would be the same as the rhetoric of Notre Dame, both disguising the fact that the fourth great thing they needed was a football team.

Michael Himes: A distinguishing mark of the two schools.

Thomas O'Meara: I came to the conclusion, as I'm sure everyone has come to the conclusion, in teaching undergraduates their required courses in theology, that they're so well educated—and society is so demanding of them being well educated—that they have to be honestly introduced to how theology thinks about certain topics. The time and notion that two-hundred-forty Catholic universities and colleges were being led down the road of religious studies or philosophy of religion courses that had very little to do even with

Christianity, much less with Catholicism, has been challenged for over twenty years. The difficulty with undergraduate education is the difficulty with education of all kinds of people, and that is that the Church has to accept the idea that new questions do not need immediately to be solved. We find ourselves in an atmosphere in which there can be no uncertainty about anything, no ambiguity about anything. For example, regarding the question of ordaining women, the discussion of the question was ended before it had even begun. There's a fear that to leave any new question open—not the question of the Resurrection or of the Trinity, but to leave any new moral or ecclesiological question open—is a sign of weakness, lack of faith, and/or of yielding to the world's ambiguity and relativism. Those are the words used. This makes education and theology impossible. Who on earth has instant access to the answer to every new moral and doctrinal question. I remember hearing Karl Rahner say that if the pope had that kind of infallibility, then he'd just open his office at nine o'clock in the morning, they'd have an appointment book, and each person would have a five minute time slot. The person would come in, and the pope would say "shoot." By noon, he would have answered hundreds of difficult questions. You can't have that approach to theology. The teacher and the preacher and the Catholic all have to understand the difference between serious questions and questions that are a little bit more at the margin of revelation, questions that the Church has discussed for centuries, the divinity and humanity of Christ, as well as questions that emerged only eight years ago. There were two hundred years between the councils of Nicea and Chalcedon in which to discuss the theology of Christ. If you have the idea that every question is solved immediately by some foreign person, and that any kind of discussion of our faith is a sign of weakness or relativism, then the devoted people in the Church would become evermore devotional and simpleminded—and that's the difficulty. A different atmosphere has to be created in which people can understand what's central and what is new, and not have the same criteria imposed for the new issues as they have for the issues that have been discussed for centuries or millennia.

Catherine Mooney: I didn't want to address the first part of that question because I don't know the answer, and I just want to say it was about adult education, I believe.

Richard Miller: Yeah, the first part of the question. Primarily, the answers have been regarding education of seminarians although Fr. O'Meara dealt with Notre Dame.

Catherine Mooney: I was thinking about the education of the laity.

Richard Miller: …the issue of the laity and how to have an informed laity if they're going to be elected.

Catherine Mooney: I don't really know the answer, but I've thought about the problem. Obviously, some education can take place in homilies, but homilies aren't really to—they're supposed to be inspirational and hortatory in addition to conveying some information. And the homily isn't enough time, anyway, to teach, so there really is no forum for Catholic teaching in the way there was prior to Vatican II when there were more devotions, and I was thinking of this during Fr. O'Meara's talk. When there were novenas and there were things like that, these were like holy lectures almost that were given on Catholic topics. And now that Catholics don't get together for these, there's less opportunity for that kind of education. Some parishes and dioceses have great educational programs, but it's very uneven from parish to parish and across the nation, and so I think it's something we just need to think about. I don't have the answer, but we have to have ways for the laity to be more informed without, of course, turning themselves into theologians. People have other things to do. But we need to know more so that we can be critical in a positive way.

Richard Miller: Just following up on that and we can maybe come back to it since many of the people in the audience are lay educators. Are there any themes that need to be recovered? Look for instance at the catechism. It's so massive. Are there any themes, unifying principles, that you think need to be reclaimed doctrinally?

Michael Himes: Very quickly, yes. Just let me mention one or two. Very important for the people engaged in educational work: the classical Catholic notion of the hierarchy of truths, the idea that things may be true but not everything is equally important or equally central, that there are some things that are right at the core of our faith and there are other things that are true and valuable but much less significant. The *Catechism of the Catholic Church* is a fine book in many ways, but one of its problems is it has no sense of a hierarchy of truths. Everything is presented as of equal importance. So the Trinity, the Incarnation, and guardian angels are all on the same level. Now, I'm all in favor of guardian angels: "If anybody asks you what Himes think of guardian angels, he's *for* them, but they're scarcely of the center of the faith." So one thing is to begin to center people on what are the core doctrines, what are the core issues: Trinity, Incarnation, redemption, the doctrine of grace. As central sacramentality, these are central to the Catholic vision. There are many other things which are interesting, important, valuable, but not central, and we need to get that sorted out for people.

Michael Buckley: I want to say one thing positive about adult education and then one thing perhaps more challenging. For the last fifty years, I've heard people moan about Catholic education. The kids don't know so forth and so forth, and when we were younger, we knew what the fruits of the Holy Ghost were and we don't know the fruits anymore. Fine. But I want to point out something: that when the greatest scandal in the history of the American Church hit over the last two or three years, I was amazed how few Catholics left the Church. Whatever process of education was going on, perhaps a mixture of liturgy and catechetics, and whether people's knowledge of the catechism may be more vague on a lot of things, somehow or other they know there is something binding to the Church in love and affection, and that this is where they find spiritual nourishment—that is remarkable. My own personal opinion is that (and you don't really know how it would come out) if that same crisis had hit the Church fifty years ago with the same kind of scandal, I'm not at all sure that age would have responded nearly as well as the present-day Catholics did. That's the positive side.

The second thing I would like to say is that, structurally, adult education is one of the most important ministries in the Church. There are so many adults who really have very little idea or contact with Sacred Scripture or with the basic themes of the dogmatic teaching of the Church. In my opinion, adult education is one of the most important ministries of the Church and it should be part of the structure of every single parish. How one pulls that off, I'm not sure, but I do think there are a lot of resources right now in the Catholic population, because of so many people who have studied theology, to allow almost any middle class parish to be able to fill something here that would do a great deal of responsible good.

Richard Miller: OK, we're going to move on to a new topic. This one is actually for Fr. Buckley. Could you please flesh out the "one, two, three" to let your suggestions move into actuality? You had several suggestions—how do we implement those?

Michael Buckley: First you have to kill a number of clerics.

Richard Miller: And in those questions there was the issue of time. How long will it take? How is it possible and how long will it take? What are the actual things that need to be done?

Michael Buckley: Good. Well, let's start off with the first which is the structure for the election of bishops. Could that be done? Yes, it could be done. It could be done under the leadership of the pope. If the pope put his mind to being an agent of the liberation, or the restoration, of the integrity of the local church, this would bring changes very rapidly. In his previous encyclical, I believe around paragraph 90 someplace, the pope asks the pastors and teachers in the Church to submit ways in which the primacy could be exercised, keeping its essential nature but adapting it to our times. My personal opinion is that one of the ways in which this could be done most effectively is, if the pope—almost analogically with what Gregory VII did—tried to foster the freedom and independence and autonomy and integrity of the local church in communion with him, I think it would go very far. Without that kind of influence, leadership, and so forth, it will go very slowly. It would then pass by another direction, which is the direction of public opinion. Gradually, there is a public opinion growing in the Church that is moving in this direction, and I think that will take time. But could it be done? Of course it could be done. Universities get presidents from all sorts of different places. There's no reason why the pastoral council in the diocese and the priest senate and maybe one other organization could not collaborate to look for candidates, to investigate candidates or people whose names have been suggested, to see what their religious qualifications are, and then submit either a terna—a list of three names—to the local clergy and bishops, or make a decision themselves. But there's a lot of ways that can be done. The major way will have to involve both a growth in public opinion, on one side, and a "conversion" of the Holy See to see that this is not the destructive abolition of control and unity and so forth, but really a restoration of what we had in the first five, six centuries.

Now, I don't have to go through all three of these?

Richard Miller: No, no, you don't have to go through all three. In line with this, the issue of the election of bishops was mentioned throughout. Fr. Buckley and Professor Mooney focused on it very much, but this is for the whole panel. You mentioned the issue, Fr. Buckley, of polling. Some people are sensitive to the chaos that goes with that, I mean, as we look to the past, we realize there is chaos in the past, so our decisions for the future will issue new chaos.

Michael Buckley: Richard, I did not use the word "polling."

Richard Miller: Just now you used the issue of "opinion."

Michael Buckley: Of public opinion in the Church.

Richard Miller: OK. I'm sorry. But the issue that's raised here is how do you avoid corrupt elections, the issue of provincialism and narrowness, the problem of people's nervousness about a church polling (Fr. Himes raised the issue of polling) everyone. Where do you go and deal with the local church and the issue of democratization which some people are nervous of?

Michael Buckley: Two things, Richard. Obviously, I can't take each single possibility in a structure like this and say I would handle it this way and so forth. I can't do that. On the other hand, I do agree with the thought behind that question, which is, there are going to be maladjustments, maladroit handling of these things. There were in the early Church. There were riots in some cities, sometimes about who was going to be appointed. People died. I don't expect that to happen in Syracuse or in Cincinnati, but I think that there will have to be ways of seeing that the thing is done justly. Of course there will be problems. I mean, there's no human arrangement that doesn't have serious problems. And you would have to see that the arrangement is such that it really is a step up. Those are all very serious questions. But if you haven't got the leadership that wants to put it in, then it's impossible, because you end up simply in a world of possibilities that has no end.

Richard Miller: That was a question for the whole panel.

Richard Gaillardetz: I probably need to weigh in sometime here. You know one of the things that's often mentioned particularly about the election of bishops is precisely the concern that you'll have politicking and behind-the-scenes stuff—as if this isn't going on now! The issue isn't whether politics will enter into the appointment of bishops. It will always, in any procedure, enter into the appointment, so it's naive to imagine that it won't enter in. The other thing is we have all sorts of models already at our disposal for this, for example, in the history of many professed religious communities that have long since used a variety of very well-developed discernment models for the choice of leadership. But beyond the question of consultation for the election of bishops is the broader question that Michael was raising about the consultation of the faithful to discern the sense of the faithful. Here in the United States we were at the forefront of this in the 1980s in the way that the American bishops set about the process of developing their two key pastoral letters in which, obviously, they didn't hand out ballots to everybody and say, "Are you for nuclear war or not?" But what they did was a very sophisticated process of listening sessions at the diocesan level, of a drafting committee that would write a draft that would solicit comments. They had the courage to invite people they knew would disagree with them and hear their testimony. They went through a long process of doing that without in any way abdicating their own authority. And they offered, I think, a wonderful model for the kind of process of consulting that doesn't have to be crass Gallup polling but is a genuine attempt to try and discern the sense of the faithful.

Michael Buckley: If I could take that from the other direction. I live in Boston, and we're awaiting the appointment of a new archbishop. At least *I* don't have any idea who this is going to be. If there was any consultation, it escaped me. The only consultation or the only discussion is about every three or four months the Boston Globe runs a story with the same six pictures of people from all around the country for which, I suspect, there's no basis whatsoever, and the opportunity that it will be one of these people is highly unlikely. So I think both processes have their downsides, but there's an upside to both too, and I think in the present situation, at least, to have had some discussion in our archdiocese would have been most helpful and most timely for us.

Michael Himes: This is not so much a suggestion of how to do it—it's just an observation which it might be interesting to recall, and most of us tend to forget. We have spoken about other forums in which bishops have been chosen, and we spoke about them in the first millennium, in the courts of the Middle Ages. You don't have to go back that far. The fact is that you know there is a new Code of Canon Law that was promulgated in 1983. The prior Code of Canon Law was promulgated in 1917, so it's not yet ninety years old. That was the first Code of Canon Law in the history of the Church. It's interesting to remember that for nineteen centuries there was no universal code of law in the Church. A universal Code of Canon Law has only existed for less than ninety years. The reason I mention that 1917 Code is that it's at that point that the current system of appointing bishops is made universal law. On the eve of the First World War, in 1914, *73 percent* of the bishops of the world had *not* been appointed by the Holy See. That's less than ninety years ago. So you don't have to go back nine hundred years to talk about alternative methods to the current appointment. The current appointment, the system, the one that many people regard as traditional, is not yet as old as many countries in Africa. It's not really very traditional. It itself is very new, and if you want to say in 1917 we tried a new system, seventy years later we could say, "Yeah, and it didn't work. So let's go and try something else." But it's not that long ago that there were very different systems in place.

Richard Miller: This again is a question for the whole panel. If a Church in tension is a Church fully alive, how do we determine a healthy tension from a destructive tension, and how or who maintains that balance? I'll give you about two days to think that one out.

Michael Himes: Since I invoke that image using Newman and Möhler, I'll start. The sign of a healthy tension is that all the parties in the tension are willing to admit the tension is healthy. That's the primary. The moment that somebody says, "No, you're out," the moment that somebody says, "I refuse to talk to you," the moment that somebody says, "I'm sorry if you hold that position; I cannot deal with you anymore" or, "I simply won't speak to you," at that moment, that person has put him or herself out of the conversation. That's become unhealthy. It seems to me that John Courtney Murray was fond of saying that one must not confuse when one says the Church is not a democracy. No, the Church is not a democracy if you confuse democracy with one of the techniques of democracy; namely, one person, one vote. That's a technique of democracy. That's not the essence of democracy. There have been many democratic situations that were not simply one person, one vote. The essence of democracy—whether or not it's a fully adequate definition, is another question, but it's a helpful image—Murray said, was "conflicting opinions locked in civil conversation," and the two important words (but everyone always looks at "conflicting") are "locked" and "civil"; that it's a "civil" conversation. People are willing to say, "I disagree with you, but I am willing to recognize that you are an intelligent and well-intentioned person, and therefore I want to hear why you think what you think, although I probably disagree with you." And secondly, the conversation is "locked"—you haven't got the right to get up and get out of it. The thing that makes a conversation or makes this tension unhealthy is the moment somebody says, "I'm right, you're wrong, and there's nothing more to talk about." At that moment, the conversation is not only uncivil, it's become unlocked. Then it's not democracy at all. So that's the first important sign.

And if I could say a quick word about the second. Who should hold on to this? This is what the magisterium is for. The magisterium is not to decide conversations. The magisterium is to make sure that nobody gets off the table. Nobody is locked out, nobody has the right to lock anybody else out, and nobody has the right to walk out. That's the point at which the magisterium functions most healthily. It's not about excommunicating people; it's about not letting people excommunicate themselves or anybody else. It's about in-communication, not excommunication. That's what makes a healthy magisterium and that's what makes a healthy tension.

Richard Miller: Fr. Buckley?

Michael Buckley: Yeah, I would agree with that very much, obviously. You know the tension is no longer healthy when the criterion given by Saint Paul for the presence of the Spirit are absent. In Galatians 5, he talks about the signs of the flesh are obvious, that is, being lead by destructive impulses within the person: impurity of spirit, anger, hatred, all that stuff, whereas the fruits of the Spirit are love and joy and peace and patience and so forth. It seems to me this problem of healthy tension and destructive tension, every religious order, that every community has to deal with that. It's not just on this kind of level within various ranks of the Church. I presume almost every family does. Maybe we all do inside of ourselves as well. The difference is that one looks in a healthy one for the signs of the Spirit. And when you can know that you've "been had," it becomes destructive when the signs that are alienating of the Spirit are not present.

Richard Miller: Another question for the whole panel is what possible structures might one consider to give responsible and effective voice to the laity?

Michael Himes: I keep jumping in first. But I get in ahead of my companions. I always thought I would be good on *Jeopardy.* Quick thumb.

One thing which I don't hear us often say enough, and that is to recognize that there are other Christian communities in the universe besides the Roman Catholic Church. And maybe there are some things we could learn from our sister churches. For example, I used to be on the ARCIC, *The Anglican-Roman Catholic Dialogue in the U.S.* Heaven knows, many of my Episcopalian colleagues would immediately say we've got lots of problems in the Episcopal Church and how it works. That's true. But they've also got some interesting structures—the idea of a house of laity as well as a house of clergy and a house of bishops. It's a very interesting notion. When the

American bishops meet, is it impossible that, just as there is a National Conference of Catholic Bishops, there could be a National Conference of Catholic Clergy and a National Conference of Catholic Laity, and that they could arrange their meetings in such a way that in any given period, in any given six months, each of the three would take up the same topic and feed their reports to one another? It's not unheard of. There are ways in which we see the Anglican communion do that at the moment. As I say, not always perfectly—the Anglicans that I know would be the first to say so. Nevertheless, it's a real structure. I think there are all sorts of possibilities we could look into.

Daniel Harrington: One other factor is the number of people under fifty-five, who are studying theology these days are predominately lay. In the future, Catholic theology in the United States will be in the hands of lay theologians, basically. I know that the Catholic Theological Society is taking this up at its next meeting, and it sounds like it's a very interesting sort of starting point for lay voices in these structures of the Catholic Church.

Richard Miller: This one is directed to Professor Gaillardetz, but I think we'll let Professor Gaillardetz respond and then anyone else on the panel who would like to. The issue is really the World Church. How do we deal with the problems in Africa that are completely different from the problems that we have in the United States and still maintain the unity of the Church?

Richard Gaillardetz: That's a very good question. In ecclesiology we talk about that in terms of the relationship between the local and the universal Church. That relationship has, in fact, been the occasion of a very lively debate among two of our leading cardinals. The tendency, of course, is to want to ask, "Which has priority—the local or the universal? Which has priority—the diversity of particular Christian communities or the one faith?" In spite of the technical debates that are going on between Cardinal Kasper and Cardinal

Ratzinger on this, most ecclesiologists are inclined to say you can't speak of a priority. You have to speak of the way the local and the universal mutually inform one another. And yet, there is in our practice, in our structures, in many ways a strong bias in favor of the priority of the universal Church over the local church, even in the language we use. I noticed this when all of us were talking how quickly we call for reform, one of the words that we tend to use is "decentralization." Well, ecclesiologically, I want to suggest that that's a problematic word because in some ways what it suggests is that the center will cede some of its authority and power to the periphery. There is another principle in our tradition we can use, the principle of subsidiarity. That principle suggests something very different. It doesn't suggest that the center cedes authority to the periphery. It suggests that the starting point is always what's going on at the level of flesh-and-blood communities. When issues cannot be dealt with at that level, then the authority moves to the broader, to the next— higher, if you will—level of authority. But the starting point is where people gather to celebrate the sacraments, to hear the proclamation of the Scriptures, to live the Christian life in a concrete way. I think we're a long way towards recognizing that. In our practice, we still think very much of the Church of Africa needing to get permission to allow the gospel to take root in their culture as opposed to simply understanding that this is the natural process of the Christian faith in which people will always take the gospel and enflesh it in their particular life and their particular culture. The question ought to be how do we discern those exceptional instances where that particular inculturation of the faith in that particular community raises conflicts with other communities, and at *that* point the question of maybe we need a higher authority to act for the sake of the unity of faith and communion ought to come into play. But our dominant approach in our practical governance is to first go to the central authority to get permission, whereas it seems to me, ecclesiologically, it's probably more sound to say the gospel is always incarnated where particular communities, families, eucharistic communities gather and enflesh the gospel in their particular lives, and the discernment about conflicts follows upon that process of inculturation in particular churches.

Richard Miller: If I may follow up on that, the issue is of not only living out the gospel, but also "the way" of our doctrine is a way in which we look back on Scripture and interpret Scripture. So how do you deal with the issue of doctrine in new cultures?

Richard Gaillardetz: That question has become immensely more complicated today than in any other epoch in history. I can read the paper tomorrow morning and find that the Bishop's Committee on Marriage and the Family may be issuing a document on cohabitation. Next week a Vatican congregation for the clergy will be issuing a new instruction on what courses seminarians ought to take. Then there will be an extraordinary synod in another year. We have been inundated with official magisterial documents at every level of the Church, making the notion of a hierarchy of truths almost impossible to work out for just the sheer volume of documents. We have papal documents that are no longer brief documents intended to clarify a doctrinal matter, but perhaps a two hundred page document that may or may not be inspiring, moving, and profound, yet raises all sorts of questions about whether this a doctrinal teaching or a spiritual meditation or a theological clarification. No period in the history of the Church has ever seen official statements come forward with the number and in the length that we have today. It makes the question "What is doctrine?" and "What constitutes an official pronouncement of binding force?" far more complicated today than it's ever been, and I think we have to address that question.

Richard Miller: This is a question primarily for the first three speakers: Please say more about the place of women in the early Church in the governance and voice of the Church and whether there were ever women priests? If others want to contribute on the significance in some schematic way on women in the history of the Church, that's certainly welcome as well.

Daniel Harrington: In what I spoke about this morning about Saint Paul, obviously, right from the start, women were important figures in the Pauline mission. If you read Romans 16, which is basically a list of names, it's basically, "Say hello to all my friends, and all your friends say hello to you." There are a rather substantial number of women there, and applied to these women are some rather substantial titles: coworker would be an important one, deacon, deaconess, probably benefactor, apostle, perhaps it seems here. So in the earliest documentation we have from the mid-50s, women were important figures in the Pauline mission. What positions of authority did they have? Well, it's hard to know what positions or authority *men* had at this point. Paul basically is a founding apostle. He goes from place to place, and if you are reading the pastoral epistles—which seem to come from the late first century and after Paul, but written in Paul's name—one of the tasks there is to set up stable local structures. In other words, the important figure is no longer the missionary apostle who goes from place to place like Paul, but rather there's a need for people who stay in the same place and oversee the life of the Church. These are men who have offices like overseer, episkopos, presbyter, elder, and so forth. In the New Testament, the only places in which the term "priest" appears is Hebrews, in which there is "Christ the priest," and Revelation, where the people as a whole are called "a priestly people." So in the New Testament, the issue of what we'd call "women priests" doesn't really arise. There's no evidence of women bishops in the New Testament period, but the evidence that we have is sketchy even for men. There's no evidence of women presbyters. There is evidence, it would seem, of women deacons. Basically, that's where the New Testament leaves the story. In the second century, you begin to get the developments in which the one who presides at the Eucharist is being assimilated to particularly Old Testament understandings of a priest as the one who offers sacrifice. That gets the story beyond the New Testament. There is evidence for women who assume a whole bunch of roles in patristic literature.

Catherine Mooney: There is a fair amount of evidence of women who were in positions of authority of some sort or other from the Medieval Period. There were powerful abbesses in the early Medieval period who sometimes were in charge of both women and men. These were called double monasteries. Virtually all of these women, perhaps all of them, came from elite families. Hilda Whitney was known to have hosted an important synod of bishops. I already gave you the example of the Beguines, but there were many other women's groups and mixed sex groups in which women were sometimes the leaders. Some of these groups are problematic. It's hard for us to know all of the details about them. I've read about groups who had women priests whom they thought were appropriately ordained. They were obviously ruled heretical and driven out of the Church. Other women were denounced for preaching, and it's hard for us to know if they were saying things which were orthodox or not because the documents that we have were written by their enemies. That's the problem with studying a lot of heresies—we don't usually have surviving documents from the people who were accused of heresy. In some cases, I'm certain they were. When we move past the year 1000, we begin to get more evidence because we have female saints becoming very prominent in places like Italy. For instance, in the thirteenth and fourteenth centuries in Italian cities and towns, women were often the most charismatic authorities. If you're looking at people who were considered to be holy by other citizens, there's a brief period in which women predominate. Someone like Angela of Foligno, who died in the early fourteenth century, had many male Franciscans following her. The case of Catherine of Siena is known to all of us. One of the things that I've worked on is taking the few cases in which we know women wrote and comparing what they say about themselves and their spirituality with how they're depicted by men who knew them. Since most of our documents about women come to us from the hands of men, some scholars would dismiss them. I don't think that's any reason to dismiss those documents. The men might be telling us the truth or the truth as they see it. We can learn a lot about these women by reading male authored texts.

But the question that comes to mind is, *if* the women had written, would it have been in a different vein? Let me just give you the example of Francis and Clare of Assisi. You've all have heard of them. Clare is often portrayed as Francis's follower and, indeed, she was inspired by Francis of Assisi, as were thousands of men and women when Francis was alive. She's called by many people—she's kind of described as being docile and Marian...like Mary. I went back to Clare's own writings, and I discovered that she always talks about herself as a follower of Christ, not Mary. But when you begin to read the hagiography that got written about her, often by men who admired her sincerely, the first few will call her a follower of Christ, then in a subsequent text, the same man will say a follower of Christ and Mary, and pretty soon she gets converted into a follower of Mary. What I see consistently in these descriptions of women is that they are given sort of female figures in which to model themselves. For instance, Hildegard of Bingen, a famous twelfth century Benedictine, talks about herself as another Ezekiel or something like that. But the men who write about her—the ones who actually made her famous, more famous than her own writings made herself—talk about her as another Susanna or another Rebecca. I think one of the things that's going on here unconsciously is that the men wanted to "keep the girls on the girls' side of the classroom and the boys..."—they were Catholics, you know! What also happens is that making someone like Clare of Assisi a follower of Mary rather than Christ also keeps her in her properly subordinate position. Because, let's face it, who's better—Jesus or Mary? Jesus.

Let me say one other word that is a little more contemporary because I've often had students who will want me to present great female figures, the foremothers. Sometimes I can find them and sometimes I can't, because we don't have the text, or I don't know enough about them, or I'm not going to turn someone into a great woman who doesn't seem so great to me. I don't think our questions about women's roles today stand or fall on some of these other precedents. I don't feel any strain to prove that there were early women priests if Scripture scholars like Fr. Harrington tell me there's no evidence. Sometimes scholars get pushed toward making up a great genealogy because as Catholics we know that it has to have existed for it to be valid today. I think we can ask ourselves other commonsensical questions. Obviously, our talk about women's roles today has everything to do with changing patterns in society at large. We're reconfiguring our relationships within marriage. This is going to be a long process. It's been going on for decades, not centuries, and we're in it intensely now and so the questions we ask ourselves now are looking at the core gospel values, and keeping in mind that there is a hierarchy of truth, what do we say *now* about women's role in society. Does it have to be that we find some undiscovered female apostle? I don't think so, but this is the kind of thing I think theologians and Scripture scholars and other people have to discuss, and I think there are lots of people just commonsensically reevaluating what we've thought. It's good to look to the historical precedents, but not everything stands and falls on those precedents.

Richard Miller: We're wrapping it up here. Just a few more questions. Is there scriptural authority for the requirement that priests be celibate? Also, what is the evolution of the discipline of mandatory celibacy of priests?

Daniel Harrington: Well, to answer the first question, no. To answer the second question, there was an article that appeared in *America Magazine* this spring, I think, by John O'Malley, one of our colleagues at Weston, that gives you the whole thing. I would urge you, if you're interested, to pursue that. It's a long and complicated narrative, but it's an excellent resource in which you would have the history of clerical celibacy from earliest days up until the present time.

Michael Himes: I would endorse that superb article by John O'Malley, who's a wonderful historian. The only other thing I would add to it is I'm particularly sensitive to this, being a diocesan priest, or as I prefer to say, a secular priest, because I think it's a richer term than diocesan priest. I have long thought that one of the things somebody needs to be doing is to carefully work out what is a secular priest, theologically, as compared to and contrasted with a religious priest. I can appeal, I think, to my brother diocesan priests here. How many times, when you've been introduced as a priest, has somebody said, "Oh really, you're a priest, Father? What order are you?" And they're utterly nonplused to find out I'm not "any order." I don't know what quite to make of that. I always tell them the order of Melchisedech. I've been around longer than any of the others.

One of the things that has happened to diocesan clergy over the course of many centuries—and really it goes all the way back to the Age of the Fathers, and you can see it starting in people like Saint Augustine—is there's a tendency to make diocesan clergy look monastic. Augustine's famous Augustinian Rule initially was his description of how he lived a life in common with his clergy in his diocese. As time went on, that "monasticization" of the diocesan clergy extends to things like requiring all diocesan clergy to pray the Divine Office every day which, of course, makes perfect sense in the superb Benedictine tradition of Liturgy of the Hours. But does it make a great deal of sense in terms of the kind of ministry of secular priests, the idea of the clergy living in common? In many places in Europe, the idea of a rectory that was built for three or four priests back in the balmy days when we had so many we were falling out of trees—when there were big herds of us wandering the prairies—the idea of a place where four or five, in a big urban rectory, priests might live together…nobody knows about that in earlier centuries. Priests had their own houses. That's where this priest lives; that's where the other priest lived. The idea that you had a common life, that you would have a monastic form of prayer, that our seminary education after the Council of Trent was largely modeled on monastic education. For six years at the major seminary, I prayed the Divine Office everyday in common. I don't think I prayed it six times in common in the last thirty-one years. You just don't have the occasion to do that as a diocesan priest or a secular priest. And celibacy came in in exactly the same way. Celibacy as part of a monastic tradition of a common life makes obvious sense. It does not make obvious sense in terms of the life of most secular clergy. It certainly is not something that's intrinsic to the vocation of secular clergy. I think there's a lot of work, both historically and theologically, that needs to be done to sort that out. When we talk about celibacy and clerical celibacy, we should always make a distinction between religious communities and celibacy and diocesan priests and celibacy. They're two very different circumstances.

Richard Miller: This is, lo and behold, our last question. And this is directed to Professor Gaillardetz but it's open to the whole panel. Should there be a Vatican III?

Richard Gaillardetz: I'm more inclined to think there should be a Bangkok I, and I'm only partly joking. I mean I think that would be a very important step for us in understanding a council as a concentrated expression of the universal Church if we were to understand that that kind of gathering could take place someplace outside of the Vatican.

There are two minds on this, and I can go in either direction. I mean one can make a very good case that the teaching of Vatican II has not yet been fully assimilated and that we have more work to do to further the reform and renewal that was called for at Vatican II. On the other hand, if you look at the history of councils in the early Church, sometimes one of the most effective ways of assimilating the teaching of one council happened only when a second council came along to formalize some of the impetus of the renewal that happened at the prior council and also furthered or moved it in other directions. And so a case can be made for that. I think a good example of this is—and this is a very simplistic typology—but one often hears that Vatican I, in terms of the structures of the Church, focused almost exclusively on the papacy. Vatican II focused almost exclusively on the episcopate and didn't really develop a very coherent theology of the presbyterate, to say nothing and almost zero on the diaconate. Clearly, I think the next council, in terms of the question of structures in the Church, is going to have to attend to many more pressing questions about presbyteral and diaconal ministry and, more importantly, misses the great dirty little secret of Vatican II. It said a great deal about discipleship, about baptism, and about the laity. It did not address lay ministry. I'm not saying it didn't open the door to lay ministry, but it did not specifically talk about the kind of lay ecclesial ministry that we see in the life of the Church today. There's a whole new agenda just on this question of ministry and structuration that another council, I think, would rightly need to tackle. And, perhaps that's the only way that we can clarify those pressing questions.

Catherine Mooney: I can't answer the question either, but I do think we should give consideration to how regular councils happen in the Church. Correct me if I'm wrong, but I think the Jesuits have a council every time there's a new Father General and the Father General is Father General for life. But at that important transition when they're going to have a new Father General, they have a council, and they can call more frequent councils if they feel the need. Well, there's some common sense in that. They're not saying it's got to be every five years, they're not saying that that might be a way to go. I had referred to that decree from the fifteenth century that was trying to ensure that there were regular councils. If we take a look at the history of general councils in the Church, we sometimes don't have a council for a matter of centuries. That seems to me to be a little bit too long. So I think we should give some attention to something that might be a trigger mechanism for saying "OK, this is a good moment to stop and reassess."

Richard Gaillardetz: If I could follow up on this, and along the same lines, one of the things that's developed in Church history and in ecclesiology is a call, and it has not become universal, for a little more precision in the use of our language in talking about councils. There are a number of people who have suggested that after the first seven councils, we should really be speaking of general synods of the Western Church and be more ecumenically sensitive to the fact that after those first seven councils, we're not talking about councils that celebrate the unity of the entire body of Christ. I think one of the real consequences of the changes that Vatican II brought about is ecumenism and the way in which we think about the profound unity among various Christian churches. If we're going to talk about the language of an ecumenical council and other councils, we're going to have to ask a lot more seriously about the question of inclusion of other traditions and how that would take place. I don't have easy answers to this, but Vatican II was a great step forward in that, at its height, we had over eighty observers from other Christian and world religious traditions. In the ecumenical dialogue, we're quite a ways beyond where we were in 1965. A recent document on authority by the *International Anglican-Roman Catholic Dialogue,* made a very bold statement in which the Anglican communion suggested that perhaps the time was right for the Anglican communion, even though we have not achieved full visible unity, to begin to ask whether it could benefit from the ministry of the Petrine primacy even now. That raises interesting questions about what the next ecumenical council might look like in terms of participation of other Christian communions. To me, the interesting question is less, "Do we need another council?" but rather, "What would it look like and what would be the kinds of items that properly should be on its agenda?"

Richard Miller: There we have it. I want to thank the speakers. I want to thank the audience for spending seven and a half hours with us. A wonderful day. I hope you have been experiencing the liberating effect of attending to the history of the Church and realizing that in many ways a tenth-century murderous pope and three popes in the fourteenth century competing against each other can in some way give us hope that things aren't so bad, and that there is hope for us. At the same time, the history of the Church also shows us ways in which we can go forward in knowledge and love to build a greater active and alive community. So thank you all for coming.

Appendix I

A Sampling of Questions Presented at the Symposium

I. Questions for the Rev. Daniel J. Harrington, S.J.

    1. Comment on the benefits of scandal—three facets of scandal suggest a good that it exists—what good does it point to in our present crisis?

    2. Could you say more about "Christian virtue ethics" or give us a reference or two?

    3. Please say more about the place of women in the early Church in the governance and voice of the Church. Were there ever women priests?

    4. Knowing that you have spent a lifetime of scholarship on Jesus and the New Testament, what enlightened thoughts might you share with us on what position Jesus may have taken toward the recent Iraq war?

    5. Would you please comment on the evolution of the discipline of mandatory celibacy for priests? Is there scriptural authority for the requirement that priests be single, celibate?

II. Questions for the Rev. Michael J. Buckley, S.J.

    1. How did the current method of papal appointment of bishops come into practice and why?

    2. In *Ut unum sint,* John Paul II offered to reexamine primacy for sake of communion with the Eastern Churches. What are the chances of our own bishops taking him up on this offer?

    3. We have heard the Leonine maxim that a bishop is to be elected by "all." Unfortunately, we did not hear the original Latin. What kind of textual evidence do we have that would indicate how this took place practically?

4. How does one decide what to utilize or value from the first century (i.e., the election of bishops) and what not to value?

5. How would lay representation to election of local bishops be facilitated? What examples from the early Church are there?

6. Do you see any hope for reorganizing the curia in our lifetime? If you know of the abuse of power, and we know this, why doesn't Rome know this?

7. What steps need to be put in motion to have the selection of bishops changed to an election by all? *[In all, about 20 questions concerning how to restore this old way of selecting bishops.]*

8. What theological differences separate us (Roman Catholics) from the Orthodox (Byzantine) Church? How did the politics in the first millennium effect this schism?

9. How does your position on "local" bishops sit with the Holy See today?

10. How would the local election of bishops affect worldwide unity and how could the process be designed to encourage unity, especially in matters of faith and morality? How would you prevent provincialism?

11. Wasn't the present system of appointment of bishops by the pope an attempt to avoid the election of corrupt and incompetent persons? What is to prevent this?

12. Does the present degree of centralization of power and authority in Rome, with the accompanying abuses, diminish the respect and obedience which Catholics would owe to authoritative statements and disciplinary norms emanating from Rome?

13. In the early Church, did the local community have the authority to appoint their own priests in the absence of action from their bishop?

14. How realistic, in the short term, are the prospects of the reforms you have suggested, since the Holy See and the clergy who now control the process would have to relinquish some of their own authority?

15. How could the potential problems involved in the election of bishops—such as corrupt elections, decisions based on popularity, provincialism, narrowness, structure of accountability, worldwide unity—be avoided?

III. Questions for Dr. Catherine M. Mooney

1. You said the Council of Trent was not merely reactionary: Was a counterreformation going on well before the Protestant Reformation?
2. What role did militant Islam play in the centralization of the Church hierarchy in the Middle Ages?
3. What is the source of the name "Beguines"?
4. Regarding a larger role for bishops and synods advising bishops in this instant communication, media sound-bite world, even national episcopal councils can be stampeded—as in Dallas, when panic-driven, public relations-minded bishops trampled canon law and due process. What would prevent this?

IV. Questions for the Rev. Thomas F. O'Meara, O.P.

1. Are the U.S. bishops and cardinals aware of Pope John Paul's Baroque influence on our Church today?
2. What place did the invention of movable type and the printing press have in the development of the Church and the laity?
3. Would you speak to what sacramental theology is being taught and/or promoted to seminary students? I see them genuflect before the Communion minister, take the host only on the tongue, and not receive the blood of Christ. This is a great concern I have about what seminarians are being taught.
4. How did the development of the "just war" doctrine originate, and how is it interpreted today?
5. Jesus was critical at times of "human rules" and the "hierarchy" of his own Jewish faith. With that in mind and knowing

he gave us one commandment, why do we have so many "man-made" rules?

V. Questions for the Rev Michael J. Himes

1. In light of the principle of *sensus fidelium*, what would you say to pastors who do not have consultative bodies, e.g., parish pastoral councils, or do not consult the councils that already exist in the parishes?
2. Any idea what a concrete mechanism for measuring the *sensus fidelium* would look like?
3. What is the state of seminary education? How can we train/prepare our seminarians to function in the U.S. Church? How are they taught to be mutual in decision making with the laity? Are they taught ways to be comfortable in their ministry with women? What is the theology of Church that is being taught in seminaries today?

VI. Questions for Dr. Richard Gaillardetz

1. The late Cardinal Dearden encouraged consultative bodies within the U.S. Church (NFPC for priests, LCWA for religious, Call to Action for laity). Why is there such disregard for consultation in the hierarchy today?
2. In view of the apparent apathy of a large percentage of the laity in the United States, what would you suggest that would facilitate the changes you suggest related to laity electing their own bishops?
3. Didn't Vatican II "rediscover" that Christ came for all people and as such was an inclusive God? If theology is "faith seeking understanding," and the Holy Spirit was given to both Protestant and Catholic, would this not tell us that they are the other half and as such should be invited to break bread with us?
4. Is there a need for a Vatican III? If so, when? Is there a possibility that a Vatican III could be held in the U.S.?

VII. General Questions

1. Realistically, how can we get the involvement of the laity back into the life of the Church?

2. How do you feel about the recent trend of bringing priests from India, Africa, etc.? Does it serve us? Does it serve those priests and their own countries?

3. What or who will be the first to change the powerhold of the American bishops, i.e., what will cause the American Church to embrace more lay power (and less hierarchy power)?

4. What possible "structures" might one consider to give responsible and effective voice to laity?

5. If a Church in tension is a Church fully alive, how do we determine a healthy tension from a destructive tension, and how or who maintains that balance?

6. It seems to me that the most destructive of sins is the lust for power and wealth. How should the Church go about reducing this source of pain and injustice?

7. I would like to hear the speakers' comments regarding other scandals in the Church—the lack of any meaningful role for women, gay and lesbian Catholics, divorced persons. How can these scandals be redressed or addressed?

[These are about 50 percent of the written questions. They represent the heart of the questions.]

Appendix II

Speakers' Biographies

Rev. Daniel J. Harrington, S.J.

Rev. Harrington is Professor of New Testament at Weston Jesuit School of Theology in Cambridge, Massachusetts. He has been general editor of New Testament Abstracts since 1972 and is a past president of the Catholic Biblical Association of America (1985-86). Among his published work, which includes one hundred and fifty articles and twenty-eight books, are the recent books *Why Do We Suffer?* (2002); *The Church According to the New Testament* (2001); and *The Gospel Of Mark* (2002, with John Donahue).

Rev. Michael J. Buckley, S.J.

Fr. Buckley is Professor of Theology at Boston College. He has served as executive director of the Committees on Doctrine and Pastoral Research and Practices at the National Conference of Catholic Bishops (1986-1989), President of the Catholic Theological Society of America (1991-1992), and Director of the Jesuit Institute at Boston College (1992-2002). Among his many articles and books are *Motion and Motions God: Thematic Variations of Aristotle, Cicero, Newton, and Hegel* (1971); *At the Origins of Modern Atheism* (1990); *Papal Primacy and the Episcopate: Towards a Relational Understanding* (1998); *The Catholic University as Promise and Project: Reflections in a Jesuit Idiom* (1999).

Dr. Catherine M. Mooney

Professor Mooney is Associate Professor of Church History at Weston Jesuit School of Theology in Cambridge, Massachusetts. Among the numerous articles and books she has either authored or edited are *Phillipine Duchesne: A Woman with the Poor* (1989) and *Gendered Voices: Medieval Saints and their Interpreters* (Middle Age Series, 1999).

Rev. Thomas F. O'Meara, O.P.

Fr. O'Meara is William K. Warren Professor of Theology Emeritus at the University of Notre Dame. He has been past president of the Catholic Theological Society of America and in 1991 was awarded the prestigious "John Courtney Murray Award" by the Catholic Theological Society of America. Among his numerous articles and twelve books are *A Theologian's Journey* (2002); *Erich Przywara, S.J., His Theology and His World* (2002); and *Theology of Ministry* (1999).

Rev. Michael J. Himes

Fr. Himes is Professor of Theology at Boston College. His books include *Fullness of Faith: The Public Significance of Theology,* co-authored with his brother, which was awarded the Catholic Press Association Book Award in 1994; *Doing the Truth in Love: Conversations about God, Relationships and Service;* and *Ongoing Incarnation: Johann Adam Möhler and the Beginnings of Modern Ecclesiology,* which received the Catholic Press Association Book Award in 1998. He has also authored several popular video series: *The Mystery of Faith: An Introduction to Catholicism* (10 videotapes, 1994); *Questions of the Soul* (5 videotapes, 1996); *The Vision of the Gospels* (4 video-tapes, 2001); *The Vision of Vatican II for Today* (5 videotapes, 2002).

Dr. Richard R. Gaillardetz

Dr. Gaillardetz is the Margaret and Thomas Murray and James J. Bacik Professor of Catholic Studies at the University of Toledo in Toledo, Ohio. Professor Gaillardetz is an official delegate on the U.S. Catholic—Methodist Ecumenical Dialogue and a theological consultant for several committees of the U.S. Conference of Catholic Bishops. In 2000, he received the Sophia Award from the faculty of the Washington Theological Union in recognition of "the theological excellence in service to ministry." Among the numerous articles and books he has either authored or edited are *Readings in Church Authority: Gifts and Challenges for Contemporary Catholicism* (2003); *A Daring Promise: A Spirituality of Christian Marriage* (2002); and the forthcoming *A Primer on Scripture, the Magisterium and the Sense of the Faithful* (2003).